Simone Rus

How To Do The First Walk of Santiago

Guide for the St. James Wak

All you need to know about the St. James Walk before, during and after your walking.

(How to do) the First Walk of Santiago

Author: Simone Ruscetta

Artwork & Cover: 24media.it

English version: Mara Moretti

Photos: Simone Ruscetta, Shutterstock.com

Copyright © 2018 Leones Books & Printing

ISBN: 978-88-943119-9-0

1st Edition: February 2018

All rights reserved

WebSite: www.primocamminodisantiago.com

to the Lions,

to my daughter Asia

and my grandparents

I always thought the Camino de Santiago was madness, until ... I did not do it for real!

(Simone Ruscetta)

If you are going to undertake, today or in the future, the St. James walking, thanks to this book you'll discover why over every year 270.000 pilgrims from every where on the earth deal with the most popular Walking in the world.

Reading this book you'll discover:

- the true reason why worldwide pilgrims reach Santiago de Compostela
- the Hystory of St James and the walking
- the different walk routes
- how to organize yourself before leaving
- how you should train before leaving
- what bring with you (and what not)
- where to sleep and eat along the way
- how to survive with a daily budget of 20 €
- why the Walk is safe (and unforgettable) even if you are alone
- the experience of other pilgrims
- what is beyond the Walking
- what I discovered beyond the Walking

After reading this book you will be ready for your Santiago Walk, El Camino De La Vida, an experience that will change your life and soul.

Summary:

A premise, and one reason	9
Introduction to "My First St. James Walking"	10
10 good reasons to make the Santiago walk	12
I decided to leave	15
And you ... why?	18
1, 10, 100, 270.000 routes (but all different)	21
Sooner! Not later!	26
The pilgrim	28
Whether alone or in a group?	31
With children, animals or bikes	35
The Main Routes	38
How to Choose Your Way:	47
Before the Way: a bit of workout	49
Yes, but ... What about Costs?	52
TABELLA	54
A Low-Cost Camino: Get to Santiago with 20 € per day	57
Slow down, breathe, live!	64
Okay, we can go!	69
Do not be afraid	71
Always follow the arrow	73
The Mochila: your new home	79
How to choose your backpack	82
Choose the right shoe!	90
How to Avoid Feet Blisters	92
S.O.S Backpack!	95
Sleeping on the Camino	97
The Albergues	98
The Hostel	103
What to eat along the Camino?	105
Pilgrim's (health) Problems	112
The Bugbear of the Camino: the Bed Bugs	116

The Hórreos 119
The Credential 121
The Stamps (los sellos) 124
The Compostela 125
The Distance Certificate 126
The Secret of Santiago: the True Reason for the Camino 128
The Arrival! 132
The Cathedral of Santiago 134
The Major Chapel 136
The Holy Door 137
The Portico of Glory 138
The Botafumeiro 139
The Masses: 142
Obradoiro SquareWe are pilgrims and we wander together. 143
The Pilgrim's Office (Oficina del Peregrino) 144
The Gateways of Santiago 146
The Alameda Park 147
The Climate of Santiago 148
The Day After 149
Cabo Fisterra 151
Bonus: the Cies Islands 155
Beyond the Way: What I Discovered 157
Voices of Pilgrims 162
Ultreya! Suseya! 185
Online Resources: 187
Thank you! 190
I AM ASKING FOR A FAVOR: 192
DISCLAIMER OF RESPONSIBILITY 193
BIOGRAPHY 194

A premise, and one reason

The premise is that toward the end of the summer 2017 I made my first Walk to Santiago.   I had just a short vacation to enjoy and did not have the slightest idea of what it meant to walk so long.

I could allow only 5 days of walking and my body wasn't prepared at all for this kind of fatigue. I chose to leave alone for the Portuguese route. Actually, in any other moment, just the idea of that sort of experience sound a real madness for me.

Instead …

Instead, the Walk has changed my life, like that of so many other people, and how it will probably change yours.

Before the Walk (to get informed) and after the Walk (for the enthusiasm that left me) I read up, collected lots of information and read hundreds of documents.

The way the Walk changed my life and the desire to share this change prompted me to write these pages with the hope that you will find all the information useful to enjoy the best of a unique experience.

This was reason.

Now we can begin.

Buen Camino!

Introduction to "My First St. James Walking"

First of all thank you for purchasing this book.

Whether you have decided to do only part of the Santiago walk, perhaps the minimum to get the Compostela (the famous 100 km), or to do it completely, by choosing the French, Spanish, English or one of the less known but equally fascinating alternatives, in this book you will find a lot of information essential for planning your departure, your walking and to live the best experience that will always keep an indelible memory in your heart and in your life.

This book was born from my personal experience, that of a 45-year-old man who has always been particularly lazy, a great dreamer whose dreams have, however, sometimes crashed against the adversity of life.

This book, or rather the Walk the book talks about, is born from a very particular moment of my life, one of those periods that, sooner or later, happen in the lives of almost all people.

I decided to undertake my Walk one night in bed (of course I will talk about it in the next pages). There is always a need for renewal and hope behind every decision to experience the walk to Santiago.

The fact is that from the very first moment (actually ... the second) in which I decided to embark on the Santiago walk, I wished to realize a book about it not so much to tell my emotions and impressions as traveller (for sure I'm not Paulo Coelho) but to share the many things I learned about El Camino de la Vida, a unique walking to the world of spirituality, personal growth and friendship.

Here's what you'll find in this book: no novel but many practical tips to live safely and healthy an unforgettable journey, that not only will bring you to enjoy wonderful landscapes but will allow you to travel to the most precious, intimate and hidden place of every human being: your heart and your soul.

Within "My First Walk to Santiago" I will tell you

- the true reason why worldwide pilgrims reach Santiago de Compostela
- the Hystory of St James and the walking
- the different walk routes
- how to organize yourself before leaving
- how you should train before leaving
- what bring with you (and what not)
- where to sleep and eat along the way
- how to survive with a daily budget of 20 €
- why the Walk is safe (and unforgettable) even if you are alone
- the experience of other pilgrims
- what is beyond the Walking
- what I discovered thanks to the Walking

:I will tell you why and how I decided to leave and I will ask you to make the same questions as I did, but this ... later on in the book.

I know that, at least the first time, the Santiago Walk is a tough decision to take: that's why I'm starting from this and tell you which in my opinion are the 10 good reasons to make the Walk.

10 good reasons to make the Santiago walk

Unless you are a trekking or running enthusiast, or a regular pilgrim ... have you ever wondered why a healthy mind person should go walking hundreds of miles away from home, with a heavy backpack on his shoulders, sleeping in hostels or places of fortune?

Of course I did it, and in the next pages you will find the answer I got for myself! Not only that: I will also ask you to do a little exercise with me.

I'm an extremely instinctive person: when I "feel" I have to make a decision, or that "I have to do something" I follow the flow of my thoughts and do what I feel is right, although sometimes things do not go as I wish.

This is to tell you that my decision to make the Way of St. James was not a long thought over choice. I just felt that this was the right choice and I followed my instinct.

With the benefit of hindsight I can say that my instict was right and now, meditating on my experience, I first decided to organize those that I think are the top 10 reasons why the Walk is an extraordinary experience to do at least once in one's life. Here they are:

- **The Santiago walking is for everyone**: no matter if you love to walk or if you prefer bike, horse or maybe sailboat, the Walk is an experience that everyone can do (and in fact in my days towards Santiago I saw pilgrims of every type, nation, age and physical condition. Listen: I have never been a sportsman and yet I have made my way without any difficulty. In fact you don't need to be sporty or even have a great physical training (although these elements can help you a lot!). One of the great things about this experience is that every pilgrim can tailor it on one's needs so you can decide the different stages according to your abilities. Every year there are also hundreds of people with disabilities along the way of St. James many of them on a wheelchair. There are various services on the way to make the trip possible and easy for everyone. I repeat it again: The Santiago Walking is for everyone, for you too!

- **It is always a new journey**: in the coming chapters I will tell you how many and what are the routes you can go and discover that the Walk can be repeated and will be an ever-new experience. You can change the route, the means of transport but even repeating the same path the emotions you will feel will be always new and unforgettable!

- **It is a journey in and out of yourself**: regardless of your motivation, it will be a journey not only physical but also and above all to the discovery of yourself and your deeper self. It will be a great way to break away from your daily routine, to look and listen to you better, a unique opportunity to test and grow your soul.

- **It is a spiritual journey**: the time you spend walking and meditating, the places you will see, the emotions you'll feel will allow you to explore your spirit, concentrate on your thoughts and your life, otherwise, impossible.

- **It is a journey into the beauty**: the itinerary along the French and Spanish roads, UNESCO World Heritage too, is a wonderful journey into nature. You will see amazing places, a varied and beautiful nature, but also unique art and culture sites in the world. The Way of Santiago crosses areas of extraordinary beauty both from a naturalistic point of view and landscapes as well as cultural point of view.

- **It is a different journey**: an experience that everyone should do at least once in life and not just to visit a beautiful European country. It will be a total immersion in nature, a journey during which you can rely only on your own strength, an experience that will teach you the value of essential needs and time.

- **It's a journey into friendship**: if you leave with the company of someone, you will be bound forever by an unforgettable experience. If you leave alone, along the path you will know people from all over the world, each with their own stories, their own culture and their deep motivations. They will be companions of a few kilometers, or whole days but will always stay in your soul.

- **It's a healthy journey**: Spanish cuisine is delicious, so you'll probably find it hard to lose weight thanks to the Santiago Walk, Nonetheless it will allow you to do healthy physical activity in contact with nature. The way you will do either by walking or cycling will force you to do a pleasant and stimulating workout every day.

- **It's a journey beyond your limits**: you will learn how to suffice yourself, helping others, but also accepting their help, you will test yourself each and every day physically and mentally. You will learn to forgo anything superfluous and slow down your rhythms, thus taking a break from your everyday lifestyle. You will discover your determination, your mental opening, your spirit of adaptation and adventure. Do you really think you'll be the same person once you'll be back home?

- **It is a journey that will surprise you**: not only will you learn to overcome

your limits, but you will be amazed at the beauty you will meet, the landscapes you will see, the people you will meet. And when you get there, you'll be amazed at yourself too.

These are just some of the good reasons why you should be happy to leave for the Way of St. James (or plan to leave soon). If sometimes you will wonder why you are leaving, or why you are walking for days and days in the nature with your backpack on the shoulders, I'm sure that remembering these reasons will bring you all the momentum and enthusiasm. For sure this helped me a lot!

Well, now that we have seen together the 10 best reasons to make the Way it's time to tell you why, on a hot evening at the end of July, I decided to leave. Alone.

I decided to leave

Never throughout my life, not even for an instant, I thought about making the Santiago Walk. Every time I heard a relative, some friends, simple acquaintances or listeners of the radio where I work to tell about this experience, I wondered what could lead a person to undergo such a torture.

Walking for days under the burning sun or under the heavy rain with a backpack on my shoulders? Tearing my feet and legs with blisters and more? Sleeping on mattresses and dorms with dozens of other people? Eat who knows what and who knows where?

I only asked one question: why? Are you crazy?

My answer was always the same: never in my life!

May be because I have always been lazy, that even though for the first 20 years of my life I have been an enthusiast camper (to tell the truth my parents are), then I appreciated the comfort of hotel facilities, or driving every year about 40000 kilometers by car, I looked like an heresy the choice to go on foot. In short, for one reason or another, the image of the pilgrim towards Santiago inspired only images of unbelievable suffering and drastic bother,

Do not worry: Life always has surprises in store for us and are often not pleasant.

It often happens that what we live every day changes and leads us to new paths, unknown to us: there will always be old things that we will leave behind and new things that will break into our lives.

Probably this happened to you too; I actually think it's valid for most people (if not the totality) facing a period of great difficulty, maybe in the past or even now while you are reading this book.

The loss of a loved one, a sentimental crisis, the end of your story, difficulties in your profession, or the loss of your job, or a disease that breaks your serenity and that of your family.

Obviously, I wish you that life will always bring the best in serenity, health and happiness. I know you will fight every day for that. You have all my encouragement, all my support, all my best wishes.

Sometimes it happens and, of course, to me too.

Actually, it was not a single occurrence to make me feel the need to leave for the Santiago walk, but an amount of different problems (personal, affective, working) that at a certain point began to grow more every day, until completely obscure my view of the beautiful things, maybe just a few but beautiful.

I remember that night perfectly.

It was a summer Sunday, late July. A Sunday night like many others.

I was lying in my bed wandering among my thoughts and worries: love and family affairs, health problems, the job, the house and bills, even what to do in my elder age.

In all this mess I was trying to decide where to go on holiday, being aware that for the second time in my life I would be alone.

I felt the need to move away from my habits: away from hotels, villages, crowded beaches, highway queues, fake fun and relaxation. I felt more and more growing the need to break with the past and change mindset and destination.

I am not a believer, or rather: my religious view matches only partially with the Catholic religion, many aspects of which I strongly criticize.

Yet the imagine and the word that best represents and synthesizes the way I thought to throw the cards on the table of my life and leave for the Walk is a word that often matches religion (although it is not my case): the call or flash of inspiration,

I swear it, I was thinking of anything else and, though I like walking, I would never have imagined I could do such a thing.

Instead ...

Instead, at a certain point words came out of the mouth, the idea got shape, instinct gave it substance, body, volume, and determination, and the horizon suddenly got rid of the clouds that dazzled it.

I have to make the Way of St. James.

And so it was.

And you ... why?

I do not know how far the reasons that led me to embark on my journey can be interesting for you and I do not want to get you bored. That's why I tried to tell you in the simplest and lightest way possible.

You might remember that at the beginning of the book I promised you that I would give you so many practical tips and very few stories.

But I have a question for you, or indeed ... you have to do it.

Why did you decide (or are you thinking) to walk the Santiago Way?

On the day of my arrival at the Cathedral of Santiago I managed to arrive in time for the Mass dedicated to the Italians (Monday to Friday at 10:45) and during the homily of the Mass, the priest revealed, or rather recalled, what should be purpose of the journey.

In one of the next chapters (the secret of Santiago: the true reason for the Way) I will tell you what is the real reason why every year more than 250,000 pilgrims arrive in Santiago from all over the world.

In fact, the priest knows it, He knows it, you know it, I know, in short, we all know that each one of us has his own motive to go the Way.

Your reason? What prompts you to face a long preparation, a tough training before leaving and then the sacrifice for the Santiago Walk?

What will drive you to sleep in sometimes precarious accommodations, in the midst of dozens if not hundreds of other pilgrims?

What drive you to give up your comfort and to count only on what you will be able to put in the few pounds that you'll have available in your backpack?

What will push you to sleep, shower, rest, eat, walk in the sun for hours with perfect strangers you may not even understand the idiom?

I know you've been thinking about this so many times.

I also know that even if sketched, you have the answer.

I also know that sometimes we struggle to be frank with ourselves and to talk from our heart and our soul, let's figure with others.

Do not worry.

Actually, I do not want to know about it.

Or better: if you want you can tell me, maybe with a private message on the facebook page or by email. In this book in the Resources section you will find all the ways to contact me.

Obviously, unless you ask me, I will not share anything you'll tell me.

In many books, especially manuals, I have often found questions like what I did to you (and you ... why are leaving?) and several white pages where the reader had the opportunity to write comments and thoughts.

Frankly speaking: I do not like those white pages in a book you paid for.

That's why I propose you to do a little exercise: get paper and pen and write the reasons that push you to leave.

Consign your thoughts to the paper, let your fingers and ink run, exactly as I am doing while writing these lines (though, more prosaically, I write it on my Mac's keyboard).

Take a breathe, focus on the moment you are living now, write who you are, how do you see yourself at this time of your life, what are the reasons that push you to bring your heart and your soul far from everyday life and so far away.

Do not write your name, nor write things that could somehow identify you or people you care about. Just do it.

Whether it's a few lines, a few A4 sheets, or a 3x3 banner (but this is up to you as it's rather complicated to carry); when you've written the final version, bend the paper carefully.

Then when you're going to prepare your backpack and you'll be ready to leave for the Santiago Walk recover that sheet, put it in a hidden corner of your shell-house, and prepare to entrust your doubts, your desires and your prayers to the wind of the ocean.

We will speak on this in the chapter dedicated to Fisterra.

1, 10, 100, 270.000 routes (but all different)

May the road rise up to meet you.

May the wind always be at your back.

May the sun shine warm upon your face and rains fall soft upon your fields.

And until we met again may God hold you in the palm of His hand.

(Old Irish Blessing)

Whether you've decided to walk the Santiago Way, or if it's part of your projects, you know that you will never be alone. Even if you're only accompanied by your thoughts and your music (I suggest you never give up music for anything in the world) you'll always be in good company.

The official site of the Pilgrim's Reception (https://goo.gl/SduLpM) every month updates statistics of the pilgrims who register to get Compostela and the mileage certificatare posted on a regular basis.

Although it is true that it is not a necessary and indispensable practice to make the Way, it is true that almost all the pilgrims arriving in Santiago once they finish their journey are heading to the Oficina to obtain the Compostela, thus releasing the data that form this special statistic.

From online data, it is possible to find out that the pilgrims of the Camino de Santiago are growing year by year: they were 237,983 in 2014, 262,516 in 2015, 277,854 in 2016 and 217,269 at 31 August 2017 (obviously missing data from the last four months of the year).

Oficina's statistics also tell other interesting truths (for simplicity, we include data for 2016): 51.84% of the pilgrims, or 144034 people, were male, while women accounted for 48.16% of the total, equal to 133820 people.

91.41% of the pilgrims (254025 people) walked on foot, 8.40% (23347 people) on a bicycle, 0.12% (342 people) on horseback, 0.04% (125 people) in wheelchairs and finally only 15 people (0.01%) who have reached Santiago in sailboat.

Santiago's Way is a world-wide experience and hundreds of thousands of pilgrims arrive every year from the world.

Here, I share with you the data on the number of presences divided by country (always referring to 2016, only the top 10 positions): the largest number of pilgrims arrive from Spain, the Iberians are 124230 (44.71%) second place the Italian 23944 (8.62%), followed by 21220 German (7.64%), 15236 citizens of the United States (5.48%) followed the 13245 Portuguese (4.77%) of 8868 French (3, 19%) 6537 Irish (2.35%) 6050 subjects of His Majesty arriving from the United Kingdom (2.18%) and after the top ten we find 4534 Koreans (1.63%) and 4441 Australians (1, 60%).

However, if you scroll the full list of nations represented by pilgrims, you will find that there are people from all nations in the world: from South Africa, passing through Vietnam, Mongolia and any other nation.

In short, the Way of St. James is a worldwide phenomenon, a real and concrete example of brotherhood, warmth, friendship, respect and love.

Did you know that the Santiago Walk is run every year by people of all ages? Of course, the leading range that of the 30- to 60-year-olds with 153153 pilgrims (55.12%) but the path is also loved by young people: under 30 in 2016 there were 75460 (27.16%) while were 49241 (17.72%) the ultra-sixties! In short, with a healthy workout and a normal physical fitness (to be evaluated only through your doctor).

In short, it is possible to say that the Way of Santiago is an experience that all people can live intensely, obviously based on physical &

psychic condition checked-up with one's family doctor.

Do not forget that you are on a walking journey, so weather, travel, and other elements may affect your health.condition may be physical and/or psychological.

As you know, the main variants of the Santiago Way are at least eight. Therefore I think it is useful to know which are the more or less frequented. These are the official data of the 2016 Oficina (the latest data available for a full solar year) .

French Path 176075 (63.37%)

Portuguese Path 49538 (17.83%)

North Path 17289 (6.22%)

Primitive Way 12089 (4.35%)

English Path 9703 (3.49%)

Vía de la Plata 9067 (3.26%)

Portuguese Path spiritual variant 2600 (0.94%)

Muxia-Finisterre 770 (0.28%)

Other Walking 436 (0.16%)

Winter Path 287 (0.10%)

Why can this information be useful to you? Because, according to your needs, it helps you make your experience better.

I try to explain you better with an example: let's take the French Way. In August there are more than 35,000 pilgrims attending it, which means more security but at the same time crowding (especially in the albergues). Are you a person looking for a crowed path? Probably the French is for you a good solution, but if you need to live intimately your experience and do not tolerate crowded places then maybe it's best to make a different choice.

In short, even the "traffic" of pilgrims you will meet during your journey is an element that can be important in choosing the path you are going to accomplish.

Think well about this too.

Among the available data there are those related to the departure cities: as I told you, every pilgrim constructs his Walk in a personal way, so even in the same path pilgrims often choose different starting points.

Here is the list of cities from which most pilgrims are coming:

Sarria 71766 (25.83%)

S. Jean P. Port 33656 (12.11%)

Oporto 17726 (6.38%)

Tui 15158 (5.46%)

León 12022 (4.33%)

Cebreiro 9856 (3.55%)

Ferrol 9478 (3.41%)

Ponferrada 8195 (2.95%)

Oviedo - C.P. 7227 (2.60%)

Valença do Minho 6773 (2.44%)

From my point of view these data can be statistically interesting but I would not use them to decide where to start from, basically they are data for a whole year! As in previous statistics, in this case, the data are in fact related to 2016.

In short, as you can see every pilgrim can arrange his personal Santiago Walk, as the variants are really infinitive. Each pilgrim goes his way for a different motivation, with a different spirit from all the other pilgrims and with a unique vision .

That is why by paraphrasing somehow Luigi Pirandello we can really say that the Paths are 1, 10, 100 or 250,000!!

Sooner! Not later!

Honestly: before that evening I never thought of doing a thing like Santiago's Way, I was not exactly that kind of person. Actually, when telling my experience to the people I know, or to listeners on the radio where I still work or posting fragments of my Path on my Facebook profile I found that there are so many people who have already made the Way but even more those who would like to do it .... Sooner or later.

Well, I have always considered the sentence "sooner or later" with great suspicious because in my opinion, sooner or later, it is a great trick. Sooner or later I marry, sooner or later I have a son, sooner or later I will travel, sooner or later this, sooner or later that, sooner or later I will be happy.

I've always been an extremely positive person, maybe too much, and I still feel like a very lucky person, was nothing else because I was born in the right part of the world.

I have the greatest respect for Life and I am hungry of it. But that "sooner or later", however, smells like a rip off, because none of us can know what is going to happen in the future. Sometimes the "you have all your life in front of you" is really up to a beautiful old age. Sometimes...

But the truth, unfortunately, is that often life is not so generous, and that sometimes a second is enough for our projects to vanish, melting like snow in the sun.

That is why if you have a dream, if you have a project it is better to try and realize it "first" instead of "then" as the perfect moment will probably never come by itself.

The perfect moment, the alignment of better events and stars is not "then" is "before".

Do you feel ready? Do you have a dream? Fight to accomplish it, do it today not tomorrow. Infact, as somebody said a lot better than me, "no certainty about tomorow". Tomorrow things could change, tomorrow something might happen (also positive of course) that will force you to postpone again. And then again.

That's why I decided that the "then" I have to use it sparingly, I have to focus it carefully and respect myself. That is why I prefer the "sooner".

That is why when I heard that it was the right time to take the Path I seized it without waiting for the perfect moment, probably never going to come.

I enjoyed the few days of vacation I had available and I began to prepare myself ... because after a few weeks I would leave!

Sooner, not later!

The pilgrim

I never thought I could one day call me a "pilgrim", but as we often could see life offers us some amazing new experiences.

The pilgrim is the person who decides, in a certain moment of his life, to travel for reasons other than those of leisure and fun. It is a journey to a place considered sacred, for spiritual research, penance or for religious reasons.

Usually, the pilgrim travels along predetermined paths in ways that are different from those he lives his daily life, taking time away from the usual activities and utilizing it in meditation, spiritual research, and often in prayer.

The word is of Latin origin, exactly by the term peregrinus, by + ager (the fields), and indicated the foreign person that coming from the countryside was forced into poverty, or poor wellness.

In the modern era, however, its use has changed, implying the condition of a pilgrim to a definite choice, that of a person who is not a foreigner but chooses to do so, renouncing material well-beings to aspire to spiritual ones. A person who, in the name of his choice, takes on the physical and spiritual risks as well as the labors of the same.

When you leave with your backpack on your shoulders you will be part of this millennial community, a melting-pot of people of different nations, tongues, races and cultures, combined with a common denominator: the search for a deeper spirituality.

The modern pilgrim is a person constantly connected with the rest of the world, able to travel with comfort unthinkable till a few decades ago.

Who instead decided to undertake a pilgrimage in the past centuries, was far from an easy life; often those who left did so because condemned by a court or as a penitent of the confessor for crimes or sins of particular magnitude (homicides, thefts ...) . Many then left (as they are today) to ask for grace, respect for a vote, or for own personal research.

In any case, those who departed were losing any properties and often had to sell or mortgage the assets to finance the trip. The return was far from assured, so that the pilgrim before his departure would make a testament and made arrangements for the management of his properties in his absence. It often happened that the Church intervened to help the pilgrim in the management of her patrimony.

Contrary to what is happening today, for centuries the pilgrims have traveled in groups: precarious roads, natural misfortunes and above all the bandits represented dangers such as to make the group journey indispensable, to support and protect each other.

On departure, the dress ceremony was completed with the delivery of the bag

Receive this haversack, which will be the dress of your pilgrimage, so that, dressed in the best way, you will be worthy to arrive at the door of St. James where you wish to arrive and, upon your journey, you will return to us healthy and safe with great joy if so will God who lives and reigns for all ages of ages.

Get this stick to support your journey and fatigue on the way of your pilgrimage to help you beat anyone who wants to hurt you and let you get quiet at the door of St. James and, on your trip, you will come back to us with great joy, with the protection of God who lives and reigns for all ages of ages.

(from http://www.pellegrinando.it/i-cammini-di-santiago/le-origini/)

For all these reasons, the pilgrim enjoyed a status and a prestige not indifferent to the point of being exempted from certain duties and taxes.

Today's pilgrim's life has obviously completely changed, adapting to our times and our cultures. I think almost all of today's pilgrims have smartphones to communicate with their own world, but also to document every moment of the trip with photos, video and reportage for use and consumption of social networks.

The diffusion of a sporting and wellness culture makes the modern pilgrim well-prepared in the body and of course also from the point of view of the increasingly evolved and comfortable equipment.

Even hygiene and health conditions have been incredibly improved over the centuries and nowadays the Way can be defined as safe and comfortable experience from every point of view.

Demonstrating how the pilgrim's life has changed from the past century to nowadays just see how the choice of the Way has become so widespread (over 270,000 pilgrims only in 2017) and transversal (men, women, young people, the elderly ...).

If the skin of the pilgrim has changed, more and more comfortable and technological, what in almost a thousand years has never changed is its soul: a soul striving to the search for the inner ego, of the most evolved spirituality. A soul that opens the hand to give and to receive, a soul able to strive from everyday life and to travel to new and unexplored horizons.

Whether alone or in a group?

Just in the moment I decided to make the Way of St. James on that Sunday evening at the end of July I was well aware that I would have done it alone. This because I felt the need to face myself and stay just with my thoughts; but also because having no prior notice myself to make up my decision, it would have been impossible to find a companionship. So I did not even look for it.

Until the age of 44 I had never made a lonely holiday but after Australia I enjoyed it and I learned that in some cases it is really "better alone than badly accompanied", so I did not think twice.

I was then convinced that it would be easy on the Road to meet and know, even for a few kilometers along, pilgrims from all over the world, each with their own particular story, with their own motivation and with the desire to share this wonderful adventure.

And so it was.

I left alone, but actually I have never been so. You can be sure: on the Way you will be alone whenever you want it. Just a "buen camino", or a simple greeting, or perhaps a question during a regenerating stop, to rediscover the true spirit of the pilgrim, made of friendship, brotherhood, sharing and solidarity.

Once at the airport, for example, I found myself in a group of pilgrims, with whom I shared entire days of travelling and with whom still today there is an extraordinary friendship. I could tell the stories of every traveller I talked to even for a few minutes.

I believe that regardless of the goal, while travelling alone we are able to discover an attitude to sociality that we often forget when living in a hurry and everyday frantic life. At home we often do not even greet our neighbour, or we argue with strangers for insignificant reasons.

Travelling alone has revealed me a side I often forgot: the importance of asking, talking, listening. Three things we usually do as little as possible in everyday life, especially with strangers.

Perhaps, as I have been thinking and talked over with other lonely travellers, it is a matter of pure and simple psychological survival, but travelling alone is an important test as it forces you to overcome your own limits, to open you up to new acquaintances, new stories and knowledge.

The Santiago Way is then the right opportunity to spend as much time as possible   with your inner self.

If you are thinking about facing your Way alone, allow me to share with you the advantages that in my opinion recommend to do it alone:

• **Choose your own stages and times**: whether you are an expert walker or, like me, a person at your first experience, you will have the ability to build the Way exactly as you want it, without having to compromise with anyone, respecting your times and your travel desires.

• **Walk to your step**: you do not have to wait for who is slower than you, or vice versa, you will not have to ask to wait for you. The freedom to follow your rhythm, whatever it is.

• **You will know yourself**: you will discover your limits (and you will most likely overcome them). Although the Way is, as we have seen at first, for all it still remains an important test for your body and mind. And it's a challenge especially with yourself.

• **You will know many people:** believe me, you may be the most timid person in this world, but you will soon learn how to open yourself and welcome new acquaintances to your life, even for a few minutes. You will know people, listen to stories, get closer to different cultures, and fill your heart and soul with priceless   wealth.

• **You can think**: I had a great need of this. We always run, always with a head full of thousands of thoughts that overlap each other. Sometimes they are so heavy, so many that you feel almost overwhelmed and you can not find a way to get out of it. Walking has this effect, helps you clear your head step by step, oxygenate your brain, stretch yourself out, see your problems from an objective view. There will come a time when you will feel your thoughts becoming fluid, and you will know which way to go. Walking in companionship is beautiful and it can be fun, but if you need to concentrate on your things, being in a group will keep you far from your needs. The Walk with its miles and its days will allow you to reflect, find moments to devote to yourself and your thoughts, will help you understand who you are, and where you want to go. Doing it alone will be even more precious.

In this chapter I do not want to convince you to make a choice rather than another, but I just want to share with you the advantages and disadvantages that, in my opinion, each of the two choices is behind.

Sometimes I think about the moments I spent with my travel companions along the Way, and I think how nice it was to feel part of a group (even as an "extra" picked up along the walk). Walking in a group allows you to count on valuable resources:

- **More safety**: though the Walking needs respect but not fear, it is undeniable that being part of a group is safer. Knowing that there are other people with you allows you to rely on help in any moment (a fall in a forest, a small accident or else).

- **Sharing**: True, the Way is an absolutely personal experience, but sharing it with other people who feel emotions similar to yours is a great joy. Relations become tighter and more solid, creating a unique complicity, the individual's questions find answer from the group. Traveling alone you will share photos, thoughts and emotions on social networks, but it's not exactly the same thing, right?

- **Unity is strength**: in moments of discomfort or fatigue and pain you will have someone who will inspire you, and you can be a friend's shoulder. At the same time the group will protect you from a thousand problems, it will also permit to save money on some common services such as taxis, washing machines and dryers ... not bad indeed!

As I told you I left alone, but practically from the very first night of my

Cammino I joined a group of other pilgrims and alternated moments of solitude (what I wanted to devote to myself and to my brain storming) at moments of companionship.

In short, I was lucky enough to enjoy the benefits of the two choices: loneliness when I needed to keep up my mind or just to stay with myself and the group in the moments when being together could enrich my day.

As you can see in this case there are no rules valid for everyone, and each path is different from the other. Reflect on the reason (or reasons) for which you want to leave, and take your own decision.

If you think it is best for you to leave alone do not fear and do it. Though, it is only up to you any choice, I'm convinced you will be back stronger, more aware of yourself and different!

With children, animals or bikes

We have seen at the beginning of the book how the Way is accessible to anyone, of course it is necessary to organize oneself according to ones own conditions, desires and needs.

There are those who go alone, and I think it is absolutely the best way to do this experience. Then there are those who are in pairs or with a group of friends.

However, these are not the only sort of pilgrims you can meet on the Path: although I personally have not met many families with children, I met couples with one or more children facing the path.

In internet I found some beautiful stories. For example French dad and mom with four little children and two donkeys walked over 250km: or a couple of lovers who met and engaged on the Way and repeated it a few years later with the two year old daughter. Then there is a mother from Verona (Italy) with her 8-year-old son: they reached Saint Jean by train and walked up to Santiago: now the young boy does not wants to stop!

The stories to tell would be so many, but the meaning is that you can do the Walk even with children from 2 years up.

Very beautiful the story of Erica, a mother from Friuli (Italy) who concludes the narration of his experience of the Way with a 2 and a half year old daughter with a sentence that impressed me so much:

"No, it's not crazy to do the Walk with a little girl.

It's crazy not to respond to Santiago's call. "

In the chapter devoted to the voices of the pilgrims you will also find his testimony.

And people who walk with the dog.

Just as for us bipeds, the path has to be well prepared for our four-legged friends: unless your dog is already used to walking for tens of miles a day, it's good to train him, making long walks to prepare his muscles, the heart and especially the paws.

Before starting the Walk, at least a week before, it's good to use anti-flea to eliminate any possible ones and check there are no leishmaniasis problems.

Remember to bring all the essential things for your four-legged friend: food (at least a small emergency shortage), bowls, leashes and muzzle (especially when you cross the busy streets and villages or cities) and a towel for when it rains.

Bring a first aid kit, the chip and travel documents, as well as the basic veterinary certificate with the vaccination booklet.

Along the way keep it hydrated and wet when it's hot, be careful when walking alongside highways or railways.

As in Italy, although the situation is improving, there are few structures on the Path that accept animals, so be informed beforehand. In the helpful resource chapter you will find some sites where to find dog-friendly accommodations.

It is advisable to have him wear special dog slippers for protection against the ground roughness. He needs to gradually get used to it, but we are sure that in a short time it will move smoothly and harmoniously. Many pilgrims walking with a dog take advantage of the opportunity to sleep under the stars, in the tent.

To Santiago by bike:

Getting to Santiago by bike is, as I told you, one of the options the pilgrim has to pay homage to St. James; in this case the minimum mileage to get Compostela is 200 kilometers.

Along my path (the Portuguese) I did not meet a lot of cyclists, but once in Santiago the panorama was very different, demonstrating how even those who ride bicycles often choose the French Path.

Regardless of your choice, the bike is quite demanding: the paths have been arranged mainly for pilgrims on foot (which are in fact the vast majority). I myself have walked in very steep and disadvantaged paths that become almost impossible to ride on a bike in case of rain. In short for cyclists there are several very difficult points where you should get off the bike and adapt to the path, then resume as soon as possible. I have seen several cyclists do this and enjoy the Way at the best The best bike to go on the dirt road is obviously a mountain bike with a good suspension system.

There is also an asphalt path, the Camino de Carretera, an integral part of the European Route: it is simple and suitable for those travelling with children. In this case, a common cycle bike with narrow and smooth tire is perfect.

Obviously at every location at the end of the stage, and often during the course, there are mechanics and bicycle maintenance workshops.

One of the problems of making a bike ride is ... The bike itself! If you decide to use your usual equipment you will need to find a way to transport it to the starting point: you can use the car, choose one of the airlines that allows it to be transported or ship it with a courier.

Another option is to rent a bike at the starting point (it's possible from St. Jean Pied de Port) and give it back to Santiago. This option is not too expensive compared to home and return transport.

Indispensable for the bike ride the usual hiking equipment: main repair kits, pump, spare air chambers, chain and padlocks and water bottle.

In the Resources chapter I will show you some useful sites for cyclists!

The Main Routes

May the road rise to meet you.

May the wind always stand behind you.

May the sun shine hot on your face.

And the rain falls light on your fields.

And as long as we meet again, may God keep you in the palm of his hand!

(Old Irish Blessing)

270,000 pilgrims each year means there are over 270,000 possible paths, each with unique features of motivation, history, path and life.

However, if we want to limit ourselves to knowing the ways marked by pilgrims over the centuries, then the number narrows considerably.

In this section of the book you will find some basic information, which demonstrate to be constant over time, on the main paths. These are paths encoded over the centuries by pilgrims.

Obviously, these paths have undergone (and will continue to suffer) the effects of urban and infrastructure planning: the construction of railway lines, roads, highways and new civil or industrial settlements has in the course of time made the original tracks impermanent or inaccessible, while leaving unaltered the secular spiritual charm of the Way.

One of the most beautiful things about the Way, from the landscape point of view, is that despite its length only in short traits the path coincides with "normal" roads.

On the way you will find path floors with different features:

- dirt routes: by far the most common ground;

- trails: especially in the crossing of forests and mountains;

- asphalt: when crossing villages and cities, practically never on the most practised pathways

Actually, all efforts have been made to prevent the road from coinciding with vehicular traffic; infact in many situations to overcome the obstacles caused by the railways, roads or freeways that frequently cross it, the course of the principal Ways has been deviated on secondary roads.

Obviously this made the trails longer and winding, but at the same time you will live your experience far from dangers and traffic stress.

You will spend most of your walking time immersed in nature: fields, woods, orchards, mesetas, rivers and anything else. Keep in mind that most of the route is right on dirt roads, many of which have been built (or rebuilt) in recent times.

A path that keeps you away from traffic will give you intense emotions, such as the colors and scents of the places you will cross.

Remember, however, that most of the journey takes place from east to west: so in the morning sunshine is behind, while in the afternoon you'll see the sunset.

Now it's time to start knowing the different Paths.

And of course we start from …

The French Way

As we have seen before, the French Way is by far the most popular route to Santiago, and is chosen every year by over 60% of pilgrims.

The French Way (or Camino Francés) is about 800 km long. I say "about" because (and this applies to all Santiago routes) it's virtually impossible to determine the actual length.

As mentioned earlier, each path undergoes variations, sometimes it is a minimal variation, sometimes the variations involve changes of hundreds of meters or more.

There are then different modes and measuring instruments, and other conditions that make it difficult to give precise answers to the question: how many miles do I walk?

The French Route starts from Saint-Jean-Pied-de-Port at the foot of the French Pyrenees, then continues to Roncisvalle, on the Spanish side of these wonderful mountains.

From here to Santiago de Compostela you will go about 780 km, crossing the beautiful and well known cities in the world such as Pamplona, Logroño, Burgos and Leon.

Basically, the French Route can be split into 5 macro-areas.

As mentioned the first is the **Pyrenean area**, where the path begins and cross the Pyrenees. To get to Pamplona it takes about 3-4 days to walk. In this area the weather is quite variable, with considerable rainfall. So keep poncho and backpack protection always at hand!

After the Pirenaic area you cross the **Navarra / Rioja / Burgos regions**, very beautiful areas, with a somewhat variable bottom, although without significant altitudes.

The third part of the French route is that of the **mesetas** from Burgos to Leon with very high tablelands, minimum or non-existent slopes, great hot summer, reduced rainfall and great solitude.

Leòn and Bierzo mountains: from León to Cebreiro pass you'll cross a mountain chain (the highest point of the route) and the green Bierzo valley with a more temperate weather.

Galicia: the last region to be crossed, very green, extensive forests, temperate climate, significantly variable weather with high chance of rainfall though short-lasting in summertime.

You can reach Saint-Jean-Pied-de-Port from Bayonne by train. If, on the other hand, you arrive from the other side of the Pyrenees, you can reach Roncesvalles from Pamplona by bus. Pilgrim credentials are available at the Pilgrim's Office in Rue de la Citadelle or in Roncesvalles.

Being the French Way the most preferred by pilgrims is, of course, the best organised with also suitable route signals. In addition to route signals, on the French side of the Way there are white-red signals in addition to the characteristic yellow arrow you will find anywhere until Santiago.

Those who begin the journey to Saint-Jean-Pied-de-Port can find the credential at the pilgrims office in Rue de la Citadelle or in Roncesvalles.

The Portuguese Route

The Portuguese path is, as we have seen, the second most walked pilgrim route following the footsteps of the Apostle James and runs from South to North, connecting the capital of Portugal, Lisbon, to Santiago.

Although is rather complicated speaking of precise distances, we can say that the Portuguese route is about 620 km long. Most of this path travels in internal areas, at variable distances from the coast.

The most frequented trait by pilgrims is the Tui / Puente de Lima part, actually almost on the border between Spain and Portugal. The reason is simple enough: starting from Tui guarantees the minimum mileage needed (100) to get Compostela.

Other rather frequented traits are those that start from Porto and Lisbon.

The Portuguese Path has several variants: one leads to Fatima and another, after Porto, allows to follow the Atlantic coast returning on the main path to Vigo.

Another variant, which in my opinion is extremely fascinating, is the so-called "Espiritual Variant". I travelled it with my Camino comrades and found it very attractive and emotional.

Why is this so called? because it follows the footsteps of St. James's disciples who accompanied his remains in Galicia, remember? We talked about it before.

Whether it's history or legend, the "Ruta Maritima" commemorates the arrival in Galicia by sea of St. James's body, carried by his disciples through the Mediterranean on the "Barca de Pedra".

Reportedly the boat with the body of St. James coming from Jaffa (Palestine) entered the Rias (fjord) in the small Mar de Arousa, then went up the river Ulla and later its affluent Sar, to dock, after a few Kms, at the harbor in the port of Ira Flavia close to Padròn. Here in the church we can see the so-called "pedròn", the stone to which the "pedra boat" was tied and anchored.

Afterwards the body was transported to the Libredón forest where the disciples finally gave the Apostle a worthy burial.

Thus began the cult of the Saint, to be forgotten along the time and rediscovered around 800 by the hermit monk Pelayo who in dream saw a multitude of stars falling in the field where centuries before the body of St. James had been buried. Immediately the excavations started and there were the remains of an ancient burial (attributed to the Saint) having on the right and left sides two other smaller tombs (attributed to his faithful disciples Teodoro and Attanasio). That field was called Compostela (from the Field of the Stars), and the building that began to rise, the cathedral of Santiago.

Taking the Spiritual Variant is actually very simple: coming out of Pontevedra, at Ponte Cabras, after about 4 km you just follow the directions of this route that will take you in about three stages to Padron.

The first stop will take you to a delightful village on the sea, Combarro, where I could eat the best Feira pulp of my life. But do exceed with the food, as you will have to undertake the very hard (at least for me) climbing up the Mount Busto. Once in Armenteira you can visit the beautiful monastery and rest there.

The next day you will follow the "Ruta de la Piedra y Agua", the road of water and stone. A beautiful path to the side of a water rig that slowly becomes a stream, then finally a mighty Galician river. The first trait after Armenteira is a fascinating journey through the woods and dozens of ancient stone mills where peasants, exploiting the hydraulic power of water, grind the grain thus obtaining precious flour.

Once in Vilanova De Arousa you can decide whether to get to Padron by land (walking for about 28 km) or the sea way. My travel companions and I have opted for this choice, and I must say that I am happy to have followed them.

If you decide to take the boat you need to get informed about timetables, as they change according to the rhythm imposed by the tides. The first part of the navigation is in the Ocean, and you will see one of the great Galician traditions: the wooden platforms used for mollusc farming (mussels, mejillones in Spanish, above all), and even the chance to see dolphins!.

Immediately after you enter the Ria de Ulla. The Ria are the equivalent of the fjords: places where the sea becomes a river, flowing among the rocks and flooding the river valleys for miles.

In this case the landscape is particularly impressive, thanks to the crosses and symbols that remind us, if necessary, the history and spirituality of these places.

After Pedron, the course of the Variant reconnects to the traditional path.

The North Route

This route begins, like the French one, from the Franco-Spanish border, though more to the north and follows, with some inside diversion, the profile of the coast crossing then the provinces of Euskadi, Cantabria, Asturias and Galicia.

Who walked this path told me that it is a beautiful but "tough" route:

very few plains, highly variable altimetry, with hills that swell directly on the seashore, many forests, few cultivated fields, generally an almost alpine path in the opinion of many.

Also in this trait, as in Galicia, there sevearal paths "rias" (what we call fjords) deep creeks that from the sea enter on the mainland, places that once were valleys but then submerged by the sea.

The climate is purely Atlantic: it rains very much, the temperatures are often cool thanks to an unmissable wind and the weather is quite variable.

The Northern Route (also called the Costa) is currently the third most used path by pilgrims going to Santiago, but was actually the first to be practiced historically.

This was not only because the ships from northern Europe could easily seap into the ports of these areas, but also and above all because in the first centuries following the discovery of the tomb of St. James, this route was entirely in territories controlled by Christians kings and princes, sheltered from the Arabs who occupied most of Spain.

When Christian Spain succeeded in expanding and conquering new territories, the pilgrims also moved, finding better paths on the French route, more efficient connections with other Spanish cities, and especially lower altitudes.

Since this route is not so walked like others, the hospitality in this path is obviously different: there are fewer albergues some of which are open only in the summer months!

The Primitive Way

On this path, the opinions are unanimous: it is probably the first St. James itinerary ever frequented by pilgrims; the name comes from its very ancient history.

The story tells us that this itinerary follows the path made by King Alfonso II the Chaste in the 9th century, a journey decided and undertaken to visit the tomb of the Apostle James discovered, as we have already said, during his reign.

Those who have experience of this and other paths consider it undoubtedly not only the oldest but even the most beautiful and exciting.

Why then did less than 5% of pilgrims travel it? Probably because it is a really hard route: much of its itinerary takes place over eight hundred meters high, with steep climbs and descents.

The Primitive route starts from Oviedo and the only big centers along the way are Oviedo itself, Lugo and of course Santiago de Compostela. The Path is about 315 km, and joins the French Path in the city of Melideafter approx 10 days of walking.

It passes through the interior areas of Asturias and Galicia, thus being far away from the sea, but there are beautiful mountains, fascinating villages and fresh streams, but at the same time you are continually dealing with **strenuous altitudes and continuous climbs and come down.**

Here too the climate is very damp and the weather often varies as it is quite rainy.

You will often walk under a nice shower, but if you like it as I do, it will definitely be very little annoying!

It is a journey that requires a **good physical preparation!**

The English Route

There are very few Italian pilgrims (but also from other countries) who decide to start on the English route, though offering very impressive landscapes and at least two other characteristics that should make it quite interesting: the altitudes are almost everywhere not so demanding (with the exception of Betanzos-Bruma trait, where in 5 km it passes from the sea level to the 477 m of Bruma, the highest point on the path) making it really suitable for all walkers.

The English Way takes this name after the British, Scottish, Irish, Scandinavian, and Flemish pilgrims reached Galicia by sea, since the 15th century, both to save time and for avoiding wars and conflicts (during the war of one hundred year, for example, very many pilgrims decided not to cross France, thus coming directly to Spain).

The English Way begins at Ferrol's doors, more precisely from the ancient medieval port of As Curuxeiras. This port, originally conceived as a fortune port in case of bad weather, has begun since the 12th century to accept the landing of many pilgrims.

It is also possible to start the journey from the city of La Coruna, far from Ferrol only 30 km by sea, but in fact the pilgrims who leave that city (and after 32 km of path are reunited with those departing from Ferrol) are really few.

The reason is simple: the road from Ferrol reaches Compostela after 118 km, while La Coruna with its 74 km does not allow you to receive the desired Compostela. That's why Ferrol's road is much more crowded and populated than that of La Coruña.

The landscape of the English Path is immersed in nature, thus an extremely green and rural landscape, with very scarce asphalt traits, but more forests, beaches and fields.

The climate on the English Path is the typical Galician one: mitigated by the effect of the ocean and characterized by abundant rains (practically all year) and extremely variable weather.

Along the English Path you'll often meet medieval mills and bridges, while almost all the coastal towns base their economies on fishing and naval shipbuilding.

How to Choose Your Way:

That night I decided I had to leave for Santiago's Way.

And that was the only certainty I had: my mind was absolutely empty!

Of course, I did not know anything at all about the Camino, except that it seemed a thing definitely not in my reach: too much effort and too much discomfort.

However, it was a good time to do it, in addition I am one of those people that when decides to do something activates all efforts to accomplish it (such as writing this book).

To make it short, I started doing what you are doing, document me and look for information.

Of course the toughest choice was what Way to do. Basically, I made my choice by thinking about some aspects: the length of my journey (I could leave the job for only 5 working days) and logistics, that is, how to reach Spain in the most convenient and possibly cheaper way.

In August 2017 the only company flying from Italy to Santiago was Ryanair, but this flight had some problems:

• Starting from Bergamo I would have to do about 200 km to get to the airport and so much to go back;

• Once in Santiago I had to go to the starting point (I had evaluated Sarria) returning, in fact, back;

• The date of the possible return was not feasible according to my working needs.

After days spent documenting through the web, friends and company sites I found the one that could be the best solution for me: the Bologna-Vigo flight and then on the Portuguese Path.

All this to tell you that many pilgrims decide the choice of the Route mainly on the basis of logistic conditions, an important aspect not to be underestimated.

The other main aspect is the amount of time available, although many pilgrims who wish to do the entire French Path (almost 800 km in about 30 days) divide it into three parts, completing it in three years.

For my first trip I chose the Portuguese route but from my point of view, the destination of the journey is the journey itself, and of course the point of arrival but any path is equal to the other.

I did not have any particular aspirations on the route: I wanted to get to Santiago, taking into account the time available and the logistics and so I did.

Different is the discourse of a person who makes a choice for particular interests: naturalistic, landscaped, historical and cultural.

In short, even in this case, the rule we have already mentioned is valid: every pilgrim lives and enjoys a path different from all the others.

Ultimately, I think that before you choose Your Way, you should ask some simple questions:

- how many days can I vacate, including transfer trip?
- what budget do I have for travel?
- is the go and back situation acceptable and sustainable?
- do I have particular interests that can make me choose a Way rather than another?

Now it is up to you: have you chosen what your Route will be?

Before the Way: a bit of workout

The path is for everyone, we already said it. But this does not detract from the fact that it has to be carefully prepared and considered for what it really is: a not indifferent physical and mental commitment!

Walking just for the minimun necessary 100 km to get the Compostela, within 5 days with a backpack of at least 7/8 kg on your back is not a joke you know!

The average distance is 4 km per hour, which means that you will walk every day for at least 5 hours, and all this without counting the breaks to drink, eat, go to the bathroom or just enjoying the scenery or refresh your feet in a stream!

In short, it is a commitment to be well organized so to enjoy it completely, without stress, without pain and without any problems.

As I've already told you I've always been a very lazy person and nothing sporty, so you understand that having decided to do the Way could not be a simple problem.

I made the simplest choice: turn a problem (my laziness) into an opportunity. And so, without telling anything to my family, I began to "train": first 4, then 6, then 10, then 12 km walk early in the morning before my daughter got up.

I understood I could do it: I used monitoring my performance thanks to one of the many smartphone apps, I felt my legs responding well and discovered every day that I could push a little further!

At that point I decided that I could buy air tickets, and that I could proceed with my choice and purchase the necessary equipment (I'll explain it to you in the next chapter).

One week before I left, I did what I consider the final test: a nice 20km walk, almost totally uphill with my backpack on my shoulders (weighing abundant 7kg) directcted to my parents' house on the hill,

Since I like to have aces in the sleeve I did not say anything to anyone, so I could enjoy their surprise. But above all I enjoyed my surprise!

Until two weeks before I never thought I could do what I was going to undertake (and still is if I think about how I was at that time) a real venture!

After that walk, I realized I could do it! I realized that the Way was at my reach. I realized it would be tough but that I would have succeeded in it!

Since I decided to leave until my departure from Bologna I could train about twenty times, for about 180 km in total, i.e. more than I would have walked on the Camino.

The previous January I got the necessary medical gym certificate, although my trip to Santiago was not even remotely in my thoughts.

In short, if I have to think about what has allowed me to complete with (immense) satisfaction my Path, I could say that it was a good physical preparation, achieved by walking longer distances every day, to reach, without too much effort, the average kilometers you would daily walk on the Path.

I used the method of SMART targets, developed by Peter Druck in 1954 that I try to apply even in my company. This method is a goal-setting system, according to Druck's efficient management of business goals can be possible only if you know their validity. To determine whether the objectives are valid, Druck has fixed five criteria, corresponding to the Anglo-Saxon terms that make up the acronym S.MA.R.T.

- S = Specific (Specific)
- M = Measurable
- A = Achievable
- R = Realistic
- T = Time-Based

Here's how our training method should follow these characteristics, training goals must be realistic, starting with short distances to not demoralize but increasing a little at a time. Then they have to be measurable: as you have now understood I'm a lazy person and as a good part of the guys I like technology, so I used to keep track of my workout an App installed on my smartphone.

You can do the same, or note all data on a diary, but it's important that you do it!

If you have a lot of time available before leaving, in the first periods a weekly outing will be enough but the advice I give you is to increase the pace a little at a time in order to be able to walk every day the week before departure (in this case the number of kilometers is not important).

As you'll have a backpack on for the duration of your journey, I recommend you, in the last month of preparation, to make a good number of daily trips, carrying your backpack with the weight that you plan to use. This will also strengthen the muscles of your arms and legs so you will start the journey with a good workout!

What I want to repeat is this: **prepare well, train, and be careful to your health!**

That walking is good to health (mental and physical) is something that everyone agrees at, but also remembers that you have to respect your health.

I highly recommend you carefully evaluate your health condition with your physician and start training according to the route you plan to do.

Prepare, train, concentrate and the Camino will be an unforgettable experience!

Yes, but ... What about Costs?

Do not run, pilgrim.

Happiness - what you will remember later - is not in the accommodation but on the road.

(Anonymous)

What is one of the first questions you usually ask when you start preparing for a vacation? My usual is this: how much does it cost?

There is nothing wrong with asking such a simple question, as travelling (for pleasure, for work or for personal needs money, earning the loaf is tiring and managing your budget is an important and complicated mission.

Therefore, before facing any kind of vacation, it is also worth checking costs and trivially understanding if we can afford it.

Travel has costs: for transfers (plane, car ...), hospitality (hotels, apartments), costs food (restaurants, bars ...) and then there are all extra costs (souvenirs, amusements ...). If we decide to leave at the time of the so-called high season, then the costs will rise further.

The transfer trip is for example one of those elements that affects a lot the final costs: despite the advent of low cost airline companies (and also buses), the transport means is always a major item of our vacation budget.

From my experience of (modest) traveller, I learned that even the simplest holidays and the apparently cheaper offers actually require additional costs not indifferent.

Then there is the psychological aspect: when you are on vacation you tend unplug from everything, not just from work and everyday affairs but also from your portfolio, often spending a bit too much, even not indispensable buyings.

Several times, especially in the most "economic" holidays, I found myself thinking like "I have spent so little until now that I can afford a whim", then I realize (on the first credit card statement) to have a little exaggerated!

Santiago's Way may then have such a lengthy course (from France to Fisterra over 30 days) that budget management becomes a rather important necessity either "before" to leave, in order to understand what can be afforded and how to organize it, but also "during"and "after".

In short, these are the reasons why from the very moment I decided to organize my Path I faced the economic theme.

Although I have no right to complain, I am constantly (as well as a lot of people I know) in spending review, as well as diet (but I will probably talk about it in another book)!. In short, useless to hide it, the theme of money is very important for me.

Before I left, I tried to analyze the costs I would face, organizing them in some major macro areas that I now share with you:

• **Transfers**, of course this item includes the main trip,i.e. from your city to the arrival one (and return city) and also the internal transfers (buses, trains, excursions ...)

• **Accomodations,** albergues or hostel?. The choice affects so much the costs!

• **Food**, breakfast, lunches, dinners, then snacks or breaks

• **Backpack equipment**, shoes, clothing and everything you need

• **Extras,** gifts, souvenirs, unexpected and out of schedule ... fix a budget

After doing this first planning of spending items I have prepared a simple spreadsheet (but also a trivial bloc notes can help you the same way) where I put the days of travel (in my case 5 for the walking plus 4 for transfer and permanence) in addition to the above items. The result is something like this:

TABELLA

Initial costs (travel + equipment)

TOTAL

What's the purpose of a sheet of this kind? To determine a travel budget, even partial and estimated.

I bought the airline tickets just two weeks before departure, and for business reasons I had to plan the return flight on a day when the direct linewas not available so I had to take two flights instead of one.

Moreover, since I never hiked before my equipment was inexistent; in short, I had to buy everything.

Why am I telling you this? Because I have tried on my skin that transfer and equipment are among the heaviest voices among those on a trip like this, I have faced one of the most expensive shoppings: the whole necessary equipment. After buying all the equipment and the air tickets (around € 500) I tried to calculate my economic needs for the duration of my journey, like this:

- **Transfers** around 100 € in all (I also wanted to go to Fisterra by bus)

- **Overnight stays,** as was my first trip and not knowing if I was able to sleep in the albergues I kept abundant: 25 € per night.

- **Food,** supposing packed breakfast and lunch and a light dinner I planned 17 € per day.

- **Extras** 100 € in all

Likewise, along the way, I have written down the daily expenses, marking them on a twin sheet of what I have quoted above, and I could effectively account my daily expenses.

With my great surprise, I then found that I had actually spent much less than what I had budgeted; in fact, and this reasoning is valid for every activity and not just for the Way, when you know what your budget is and keep it under control you are instinctively brought to be more careful and parsimonious with regard to your expenses.

Obviously I do not know where you live, nor which city you are you going to start your journey and I can not even know if you already have the equipment you need for your walking. That's why I can not help you no further.

BONUS - Save on flights

Thanks to the advent in the last decades of dozens of low-cost airlines it is now possible to travel at extremely unthinkable costs up to a few years ago, and these companies often make it possible to reach locations that are often alternative to mass tourism.

Saving on air travel today is possible.

Buy your airline tickets with good advance, maybe by taking advantage of one of those promotional campaigns that often airline companies (even low-cost airlines) spread to fill their flights.

As you know, to determine tickets cost airline companies use automatic software that modify the cost of your journey on a continuous basis, this means the price you find in a certain moment can change within a few seconds!

Personally, I've been using low-cost over 10 years and I've done dozens of trips with these companies, always finding me great. So, thanks to my direct experience, the research I've found on various online travel forums, these are the "rules" that I usually apply when I need to buy tickets online for a low cost trip:

• **Look for at least three offers:** do not stop at the first one you find;

• **Do not stop at the cost of the flight**: also evaluate additional costs that almost always are gradually added during your booking: priority check-in, extra or oversize luggage, insurance, payment fees, etc. Sometimes these items affect the cost more than the rest of the ticket!

- According to some research, **the best time to find the best rate is 21 days (3 weeks) before starting**. According to those who made this research it is not advisable to book flights too long before: from the studies it seems that six months before departure the average ticket price is higher than almost 20%!

- Set the alarm clock to book your flight: **it seems the more convenient time is 23pm.** Avoiding the early morning hours (8am to 12pm) should help save you more than 30% on the ticket price.

- Airlines, websites and tour operators update pricelists and offers at certain times of the year: **January is the best month to book a trip.**

- On the weekend the prices really increase, so better to book during the week. But **the best day to look for online offers is on Tuesday**.

- If you have time and do not mind staying in the airport for a time you may also consider the possibility of taking more flights: some portals like skyscanner allow this option and the savings can be really high.

To save you additional money, you can organize your backpack luggage to meet the weight and measures required by the low-cost companies, so you do not have to spend extra money. On the other hand then, as we have already seen in the chapter devoted to the mochila, limiting the weight is also fundamental for the Way, so try to respect the limits.

In September 2017, the rules imposed by Ryanair (one of the most used by Italian pilgrims) stated that "Every passenger who has made a priority shipment reservation or purchased a Plus / Flexi Plus ticket can carry a hand luggage of not more than 55 cm x 40 cm x 20 cm and 10 kg, plus a small bag (such as a purse or laptop bag) of a size not exceeding 35cm x 20cm x 20cm". Of course before buying your ticket you will have to check the conditions applied.

An additional advice, especially if you are a keen raveller, is to make an all risks insurance for trip or holiday with a yearly coverage policy: on average it is much less expensive than a single trip one and provides more and better protections.

A Low-Cost Camino: Get to Santiago with 20 € per day

The Way will teach you (or will remind you) to recognize the superfluity and to avoid it, it will teach you to concentrate on the essentials, giving up all those things that, just because they can not stay in your backpack, prove to be not indispensable at all.

Ever since, the figure of the pilgrim is matched with the image of a person with measured economical means and with minimal necessities.

In this chapter **we will then see how to make the Santiago Way with a very minimal daily budget: 20 €.**

I fixed this budget because I find it symbolic but real: it means spending little but without renouncing anything really essential. Obviously you will not live in luxury but you can make a very spiritual and comfortable experience.

Does it look impossible to you? The good news is that it is really possible, provided you accept the pilgrim's life of course!

As I told you in the chapter "Yes, but ... what about costs?" before leaving I had set a prime budget, starting with a prudent calculation of the expenses I would have to face. Well, not only I found out that I had spent less than what I expected, but I realized I could spend even less!

It's not just a matter of money, mind it.

It's a matter of new attitude.

The pilgrims who in ancient times used to travel the Camino lived for weeks in semi-fasting conditions, and one of the conditions they had to respect was also to give up their vices (smoke, alcohol, etc). It was, in short, an experience of deprivation, fatigue and suffering, a Camino of spiritual rebirth.

Today, of course, things have changed, just as the way pilgrims walk along their path. But what remains unchanged is the spirit of a journey like this, and the new perspectives that it leaves inside each of us.

It's not just a matter of money, believe me. Thanks to the Way you will learn the art of the essential (and the well-being that comes from), you will learn to live with a new and more placid pace. You will learn to slow down and concentrate on important things, leaving the useless and superfluous behind you.

So, even saving, choosing to carefully handle your money falls within the philosophy of the Camino, and it may be one of the many legacies of this experience for your spirit and new self.

Although we are more than used to any kind of comfort which we find difficult to give up, the truth is that we are animated by an ancestral survival instinct that is capable of making us fit, faster than we can think, to any situation. On the other hand, it is enough to think of the facts of the daily news to understand how man even in the most tragic situations can find the force that allows him to react even to the most extreme conditions.

Let's go back to the theme of this chapter, and find out together how to complete the Walk with 20 € a day. Of course, this cost does not take into account travel expenses to and from your city of origin to the place you leave for the Way or for equipment expenses.

Here I will only talk about the daily expenses necessary to reach Santiago, so in this chapter we will see how to manage our Walking experience with a budget of 20 € per day, which will be enough to cover these expenses:

- **Overnight stays**
- **Foods**
- **Extras**

The first item I talk about is **overnight stay**: we have already talked about the Albergues and the Hostels in the previous chapters, so now you are already prepared on this topic!

Obviously to keep under $ 20 a day the first thing you have to avoid are the Hostel (our hotels, sjust to remember it again).

Along the Camino there are welcome solutions of all kinds and price, but also within the Albergues the differences can be remarkable, ranging from 15 € to 6 € and you may find those who accept donations.

I open (and close quickly) a small parenthesis: I think it is right for pilgrims who really have little (or no) economic availability to be hosted for free by the Albergues. So let's avoid asking for free hospitality. I think that either me but even for you do not need such a hospitality, isn'it?.

What we can do to save money is to look for an Albergue with lower rates, and from my research I have found that there are so many (especially in some cities) that have rates in the order of 5/8 € per night. Obviously these Albergues do not include breakfast, and maybe they are temporary facilities (municipal gyms run by associations or sports organizations) but they offer the essential comforts.

I have seen hundreds of pilgrims sleeping in bedrings and mattresses in temporary accomodations, yet the next day they were well rested and smiling!

After all that is why sleeping in a municipal gym on mattresses and bridges can be a further experience enriching your Way, without impoverish your wallet!

I would say that by making an average of the less expensive Albergues (6/8 €) and those with normal prices (between 10 and 15 €) we can think of **a realistic average of 10 € per overnight stay.**

A choice not only to save money but also and above all to learn (or remember) a new attitude, looking for the essentials.

Another key item for our daily budget is the one related to our **food**. Even though the Walk is an experience based also on deprivation and semi-fasting, this is not the best time to be on a diet!

Instead, it is necessary to nourish properly and regularly, so that you can face this hard experience in the best of your physical and, of course, mental forces.

Therefore, **food** has a very important aspect in your Camino: you will have to feed yourself the right way, suitable to your health and lifestyle. If you are following special medical treatments or dietary regimens examine the matter with your specialist!

In principle to feed properly we should make at least 5 meals a day:

- Breakfast

- snack in the middle of the morning

- lunch

- snack in mid afternoon

- dinner

This is valid for most people and for most occasions, especially for the moments of life in which we have to face intense physical tests such as those related to, for example, the Way: walking for hours with a backpack on one's back is an activity which entails considerable energy consumption and considerable fluid consumption.

Personally, I have followed this simple food scheme every day of my journey (telling me the truth has finally become my food style), succeeding to manage my energies and my well-being.

In this chapter, we treat the argument of keeping daily spending below a certain limit (the 20 € that we have already mentioned). If you remember we've already spent 10 € for the overnight stay, so our remaining budget is another € 10. How can we feed ourselves with such a figure outside far from home?

Simple: with our spirit of adaptation and with a pinch of organization.

Do you remember what we said when we talked about the albergues? Most of these facilities also have a kitchen equipped with the necessary to prepare a meal, so why not take advantage of it?

A good way to save money and enjoy the Way, feeding properly and using the Albergues' services is just that: buy something each day to prepare your meals in the hostel.

After a day of walking, on your arrival in Albergue take a shower, rest and when you are ready go for a walk and enjoy the city where you stopped. Find a grocery store, schedule evening meals and the next day (dinner excluded) and buy the necessary.

When you come back to Albergue use the kitchen to prepare your dinner: a pasta package and a simple sauce (or meat) are a simple but nutritious and cheap meal, as well as a time of conviviality that if shared with other pilgrims will be extraordinary. Sharing a common space like a kitchen and even having a meal with other pilgrims will be an experience that will enrich you with many stories, new friends and emotions.

The morning, allow you an energy breakfast, maybe with a couple of eggs with bacon. It's true: we Italians are not very used to continental breakfasts, which instead can become a good everyday habit even when you come home.

I reveal you a little secret: in Modena, my city, one of the traditional breakfasts is the fried leavened pasta with salami (raw or cooked ham, mortadella, pork greaves, and many other salami). A peasant tradition that allows you to start the day with a robust amount of energy!

Another little secret: on my return from the Camino I continued with a "salted" breakfast! And so after my morning workout (15km a day 4 times a week) I enjoy one, at least for me, spectacular breakfast with scrambled eggs and ham, omelettes, smoked salmon or chicken breast. I feel satiated but light, and in the evening I can have a really light meal.

But let's go back to the money question. Buy what you need for the dinner and breakfast (which should grant at least 20-30% of daily calories) but also think about the two daily snacks: you need something energetic but light to digest and easy to assimilate. In this case bananas, energy bars or dried fruits (almonds, assorted mixes) would be optimum: they cost a little and give you the right energy!

As far as lunch is concerned you can buy something when stopping at one of the thousands of areas avalaible on purpose along the way. Bread and iberian ham are a great and tasty solution, but you could also prepare an omelette in the morning at Albergue and make a nice sandwich, or ... You understand, the only limit my be your fantasy!

If you usually shop when you are at home, it will be easier for oy: get organized, buy the necessary, do not waste anything, in case buy something with your travel companions. You will be able to spend no more than 6 € per day eating varied and complete.

Another fundamental theme is water. Drinking a lot and staying hydrated is important to complete the path in health and well-being. Keep constantly and correctly hydrated! Even water but rightly (keep in mind a couple of liters a day) has its cost but the good news is that on the paths you will often find public fountains where you can fill your bottle with fresh, free, good water and obviously absolutely potable (always remember to check). During my journey I never bought a bottle of water: whenever I could, I filled my 1.5 liter bottle and enjoyed the fresh water of Galicia!

To what extent of the budget have we reached? 10 € per day for overnight stay and 6 € for food. At this point 4 € per day (always on average) remain. They are the ones you can use for small extras: from souvenirs to you to small presents for friends and relatives.

It may look a small budget, but always remember that every purchase will have to find a place in your backpack, that you are in "pilgrimage mode" and that gifts should have more of an emotional function than practical.

As to me, I brought the shells collected in Fisterra to my loved and friends: a very symbolic gift, absolutely unique as it can be a shell different from the other and, moreover, at no cost.

To my daughter I brought a small pendant cross purchased for a few euros in a monastery, and the pilgrim concha (€ 1). Then I bought some badges or stickers with the famous yellow arrow for some other friends.

In short, with a few euros you can also manage the budget for souvenirs and extras. Among the extra costs consider the € 5 of Compostela and the certificate (€ 3 if you do not want the pipe that keeps them).

There will be days when you will spend more and others when you spend less, there will of course be the days when you would prefer a good meal in a restaurant; let me say that certainly you have fully deserved that and you do well to concede it.

With this chapter I hope I have helped you understand how to organize and manage your Camino with an extremely limited budget, but use this chapter only as a mental exercise to understand how to concentrate on the essential can be for anyone a great personal and spiritual growth tool.

Slow down, breathe, live!

Who knows: maybe your day is like mine: you wake up early, give a glance to social and phone, you quickly wash, have breakfast even faster and then leave for a long day of work or study. Then back home, when everything is okay you can spend some time on your hobbies, a fast dinner and then in bed.

And so every day.

Have you ever felt like the famous hamster running from morning to night inside his wheel? I did, and it is a feeling I do not like at all.

I have always worked at most of my chances, I have always tried to allow me the things I felt important, but I always heard somewhere a voice saying "Simone, where are you going? What's the us of all this?".

Like everyone else, I have always tried to listen as less as possible to that voice, because like everyone else I'm used to asking more and more to myself and to the people who are next to me. Everyone is increasingly used to seeking confirmation of one's lives and value through things, but they deprive us of valuable time and energy.

Due to human nature, or somehow for the solicitations of advertising and society system, we are led to do like animals when they go to hibernation, to accumulate more and more: the new smartphone, the new car, a larger house, new and brand clothes.

Having these things means, however, to work more and more (obviously unless you have a wealth that allows you to have plenty of free time), run even faster, and occupy every second of our time with something to do.

How many clothes do you have in the closet, which you do not use anymore? How many objects are in your life that you could give up with no problem? Do you really need all the things for which you enter every day in your wheel?

Do you smell like a hamster? I do!

About smell, I have a question for you.

Do you remember the scent of fresh flowers, those in the fields? Do you remember the flavor of the blackberries you find among the brambles, or that of apples, peaches, grapes and fruits just picked from the tree?

I'm not talking about the perfect fruits with shining colors you find in the supermarket, I'm talking about those fruits that may be dented but have the genuine flavor of the freshly picked fruit, I'm talking about the fruits you could receive as a gift on your Way, from the wonderful people of Galicia.

Do you remember the color of dawn? The silence you can listen to before the sun rises?

How long have you dived your feet in the fresh water of a mountain stream?

How long have you been walking under the stars, or under that rain that washed all the dust, from the earth and from your soul?

I want to tell you about this little experience that I lived while preparing and training for my journey.

You should know that my maternal grandparents lived in a small village in the Apennines of Modena, in a house wherel can often live in with my family.

Since I was born, now 45 years ago, I made the road to that house hundreds if not thousands of times, obviously always by car.

I thought I knew every centimeter, every curve, and every subsequent straight of that road, I thought I knew every tree, and every house.

I believed this until I slowed down.

One day, one Sunday afternoon, one of those days of August when in the Padana plain comes quietly beyond 34 degrees, I decided to do the last truth test about my workout. I wanted to understand if I was able to carry a backpack, walking about 20 km, with a good slope (a 400 meter difference).

In short, I walked the same road that for 45 years I did by car.

In short, I slowed down. And I breathed.

You've already figured out how it's over: that same road has taken on new shapes, new colors and new fragrances. Those known curves have taken on new geometries, those climbs new efforts, and every inch of those 20 kilometers has become new, as the pace that walked it.

I heard the noise of the woods, the smell of wood and grass, I saw that dry route that is usually a river, I saw the traces of roe deers that cross the woods and the road to get to the river and drink.

The same road was a very new one

So little but enough.

No matter what your life is now, how your life will be before taking your Camino, but know that the Way will change it, and I'm convinced for better.

No matter what route you'll choose, no less how many days you will be walking, 5 days (little more than the minimum necessary) have been enough for me to live and bring home an experience that will always stay deep in my soul.

During the Camino you will be with yourself every second, and the path, whether you want it or not, slow down your rhythms, gently absorb the vortex of your life, will make you find a step that you probably do not know or forgot, and you will find a new breathe.

Even after a few miles you will learn to look around in a new way, observing the details that we have forgotten, like flower blooming, the fruit on the trees, the rivers you will meet along the way.

You will realize how many animals you will meet around you: the dogs and cats of the houses and the farm animals along your way.

You will look with new eyes any landscapes that will remain in your spirit memory. You will observe how sunlight changes in the day, how clouds run over you, and how the sun moves from dawn to sunset.

Are these aspects so foregone? Yes.

Do you need to walk to Santiago to try them out? No.

But as long as you are home you are in your own environment, you are immersed in your world and in your rhythms, and are turning your wheel.

I began to feel the change growing within me already before I left while I was training. The Camino did the rest: to know that I had to travel at least twenty miles in a single day, and tomorrow would be the same as the day after tomorrow and so on with gentleness and discretion it made me slow down.

Bringing a weight on my shoulders has slowed me down, my want for enjoying the landscape slowed down. To be honest also the break for a cerveza with bocadillo slowed me down!

Thanks to slowing down I could breathe! By slowing down was as if my hamster wheel had somehow unrolled, and instead of being always stuck on myself, I had allowed me to move on, finding a new way. A way made of colors, sounds, silences, foreign words as "buen camino" said by travellers from all over the world, smells (good or bad that they were) and new landscapes.

By slowing down I have been able to realize how much we leave behind us each day, often running without a goal. By slowing and breathing I started to hear sounds and scents, and my numb and bored senses awakened.

By slowing down even thoughts also began to diminish their swirling intercession, leaving space for long moments of meditation and mental relaxation.

By slowing down I discovered to be alive. Not in the biological sense, of course, as I was discreetly aware of it before.

Spiritually alive: with thoughts able to move fluid, my legs able to take me far away, my shoulders able to bring my house. The heart able to bring myself and help those who needed it, the pride capable of asking for help.

For this reason, I suggest that you welcome the gifts of the Camino: you will remember (or discover) the slowness, the pleasure of supporting your natural rhythms, breathing deeply, you will find a new self that, I wish you from the depths of my heart, you will preserve them in your mind and heart forever.

The Camino will teach you (or will remind you) to slow down, to breathe ... To live!

Okay, we can go!

My good friend, now that we know each other better; now that you know why I've decided to make my Camino and you to leave for yours; now that I have shared with you the true reason of the Way and its legendary and millenary history...

Now we can start this wonderful journey!

A trip, I'm ready to bet, that will mark your life forever, as it has marked mine and that of the hundreds of thousands of people who face it every year.

However, I am convinced that any travel should be very carefully prepared, especially those that involve deep changes of one's habits, rhythms and mentality.

Otherwise you run the risk of transforming what might be a wonderful experience in a nightmare, a time of rebirth and growth in something disappointing and painful.

And, believe me, I would never wish it happens to you.

That is why from now on we will focus together on all those news, information and advice useful to know and to keep in mind to better organize Your Camino, a travel that will be unique, even if you do it with your friends, with your partner or with some of the more than 250,000 pilgrims who travel it every year.

In the next pages, I'll talk to you about the different Routes, and you can find the complete maps on my site (and on my Facebook page).

You will discover with me how to prepare yourself physically (and mentally) at the strain of the Way, for walking a few miles from time to time is a quite different matter than walking every day for tens of kilometers.

I will then talk about how to organize your "home" for the Camino, i.e.

the backpack, and how this will affect your well-being during the Way, but also how it will likely bring you to see things in a new light.

I will talk about how to choose the items that will accompany you every day, choices that seem trivial but that will allow you to be (and above all feel) essential, and completely sufficient to yourself. Then I will tell you how to organize your path with a budget of 20 € per day, a very important experience, and not just for your wallet!

It is not over: we will talk about Albergues and hostels, how to feed, how to avoid (or how to deal with) feet blisters and the pains of the Way, but also bed bugs (one of the nightmares of the pilgrims) and then Capo Fisterra and much more.

Are you ready?

Well … Buen Camino! Ultreya!

Do not be afraid

(but be cautious)

One of the main fears of those who are about to go on the Camino (or who wants to do it but is still undecided) is obviously about safety.

I may suppose it's because walking hundreds of miles walking on a foreign land making the life of the hiker is an activity which can inspire, perhaps unconsciously, precariousness, problems and imminent tragedies.

In the past this could be the case: over the centuries, many pilgrims have been victims of fraudsters, thieves, natural misfortunes and accidents, but with the improvement of travel and environmental conditions things have greatly improved.

These last troubled years are teaching us how the "zero risk" is absolutely non-existent, just think of what has only happened in recent years in major European capitals. Thinking of not taking any risk while travelling is just a chimera, but the same is true within the four home walls.

Every year there are more than 250,000 pilgrims travelling the Camino in one of its many variants, and each of these people walks for hundreds of miles and dozens of days.

With such high numbers, and such an impressive flow of pilgrims, it is obvious that inevitably there are accidents of some gravity, but just the numbers, however, tell how statistically the Way is an experience that requires attention and respect, but basically safe.

For example, the Francigenanews.com website reports that from 1986 to 2017 a number of 191 pilgrims lost their lives along the way, of which 9 were Italians (you can read here: https://goo.gl/qvKUaM). The site reports that the main causes are acute (heart attack and ictus), heat stroke, road accidents and deadly falls.

Even the Camino asks for caution, attention and respect. The same precautions, the same attitudes that apply to every trivial activity, from the trip to the shopping in the home market, to the walk in some not very prestigious neighborhood in your city.

You should pay attention to vehicles, road rules, limit the use of music headphones as much as possible; remember that paths, woods and dirt traits though comfortable can hide some danger every centimeter.

In short, you need to deal with the Camino for what it really is: a long journey immersed in nature and in countryside, a path that needs your concentration, attention, and prudence.

Then save the emergency number that (as in almost all of Europe) is 112, but also these other numbers:

- **Guardia Civil** (Civil Guard)   >>> **062**

- **Policia** (National Police) >>> **091**

- **Bomberos** (Firefighters) >>> **080 or 085** (it changes depending on the region)

- **Embassy and Consulate for your Country**

My experience was that of a totaly safe and quiet trip, and even the very high number of pilgrims travelling alone (including a lot of girls and women) made me feel this experience as definitely safe and devoid of particular risks.

But it's my experience, realized with the same attention and prudence that, as a lone traveller or not, I also had in Australia, New York, Rio De Janeiro or in all the many other trips I have done!

Never be afraid to leave. But respect yourself, the environment, and the people around you, be cautious, with your eyes and ears always open and with respect for those who, after all, travel to other people's homes!

Always follow the arrow

(the yellow one) ...

Dreamers follow the moon and the stars, hoping to give shape and substance to their dreams, but the pilgrims seek the substance of their walk and orientation for their steps in the yellow arrow or, alternatively, in the scallop shell visible almost everywhere: on the walls, on beautiful hand-made tiles, on roadstones along the way.

I have so many indelible memories of my Camino, but one of the main and the first one, concerns my day in Vigo.

Once in Vigo I had to take the train to go to Tui, but actually I took the wrong convoy and I found myself in Pontevedra (I went towatrd North instead of South). Back to Vigo how often I do I followed my instinct and decided to try to reach a group of pilgrims met the evening before at the airport. The fact is that, coming out of the station, I started walking with my backpack on my shoulders in search of the Way.

Time a few minutes and I began to understand how the Way is rooted in people living along the Way of St. James.

An old gentleman was talking quite breathlessly with a policeman, and it seemed like a rather overwhelming discussion when at a certain point he interrupted his interlocutor, came up to me, widened his arms and his smile, and asked me, "Looking for the Way?".

And then he pointed me the way, gave me a pat on my shoulder and greeted me with the most traditional "Buen Camino" with the largest of smiles!.

Walking on the Path, this scene will happen to you tens, hundreds or thousands of times, a bit because sometimes you will go wrong, a bit because ... After all, it's so nice to greet each other, isn't it?.

In fact, getting lost on the Way is not easy: the hundreds of thousands of pilgrims who each year, for centuries, travel through the streets toward Santiago can rely on a network of reports of all kinds as nowhere else in he world.

At every cross, the yellow arrows and directions are uncountable, as well as the scallop shells drawn on the walls, signs, garbage cans, and any other object that can host the famous symbol of the Compostela pilgrim.

I told you that the indications to arrive in Santiago are so many and different in shapes, so I think it's worth it to summarize them, at least for the most frequent:

• The yellow arrows and the signs on the ground (always yellow) are the most popular indications, often in the crosses there are different ones.

• You will find very often ceramic tiles with blue background and shell in yellow. These tiles are vell walled on the facades of the houses on the way.

• Less frequent of arrows and tiles there are also concrete roadblocks on which is shown the shell or a walled tiled or bas-relief; almost always the roadblocks indicate the missing distance on arrival. On these handwork often pilgrims leave bills or objects (I have seen stones more often) witnessing their passage.

• Road signs of various shapes

• Stone slabs pointing to the next villages and distances

I could say that once you found your starting point you could almost do all the Camino simply following the directions available, so widespread and present.

You will nevertheless lose or miss a yellow arrow or a scallop shell, but in that case do not worry: you just can ask the first passer-by, the first motorist or even ring at the doorbell of the first house you will meet.

You will be amazed at the kindness with which anyone will help you, even offering you (as has happened to me) a glass of fresh water or some fruit.

Sometimes "getting lost" (or rather, getting out of the Way) can be a choice and not a mistake. Most of the Path is on dirt roads, often close to inhabited towns you may just can see passing by. From time to time you may need (or may be useful) a small distraction, or a break, and then concede it!

Once a day, I stopped, alone or in company, for a *cerveza* break! A cool beer, accompanied by a small *bocadillo*, or a small *tapa*. All for a figure that has never exceeded 2 €! Here, another thing that surprised me is how much the life of the pilgrim is economical, and the prices are at the reach to everybody.

Listen, once, I stopped in a bar/grocery at the edge of the Camino and with less than 3 euros I bought bread (Galician bread is fantastic) and raw ham for me and my 7 companions! Yes, only a bocadillo but in comparison to the cereal bars we've been fed for days, it seemed like a starry chef!

After all, sometimes getting lost can be a good way to find precious treasures, as well as yourself and your own way.

... and the Scallop Shell!Prepare to see scallop shells everywhere, and do not worry if you can see them in the Pyrenees' woods or among the thousand locations distant dozens of kilometers from the sea but still walked by the Pilgrims addressed to Santiago.

Over the centuries, the scallop shell (Spanish concha) has become, like the yellow arrow, one of the main symbols of the Way of Santiago, to the point that you will find it replicated in an infinite number of signals, to address you to the Way but also, inevitable, on pilgrim's backpacks.

The typical shell that you will find anywhere is the classic scallop shell, adorned by the typical symbol of Santiago. Even nowadays every respectful pilgrim has one attached to his backpack.

In fact, the tradition of the shell is very old and I will shortly tell you about its legend. From very ancient times the pilgrims travelling on the Way to Santiago used to complete their journey to Fisterra (Finisterre), which at that time represented the end of the known land.

Here they used to take off and burn their clothes, and after immersing in the ocean for a purifying bath they wore a white tunic. This ritual, codified over the centuries, was completed by attaching on a hat or coat a shell picked up on Fisterra's beach.

The scallop shell was therefore a proven proof that the pilgrim had actually arrived at the place where the earth ended and that he had actually visited St. James's tomb.

The scallop shell during the Middle Ages had become such an important symbol as to represent a true certification that could guarantee exemption from duty, fees and taxes!

Many sources, including the Alteia website (you'll find the link in the resource chapter), report of a very interesting legend that is indissolubly linked to the tradition of the scallop shell.

We have already seen how, after his decapitation, St. James's body arrived in front of the coasts of Galicia at the height of the Cíes Islands.

When they arrived at the mouth of the river Vigo, the disciples of Santiago attended a wedding ceremony that was taking place on the seashore. To draw their attention was in particular a game that consisted of riding on a horse while the rider launched in the air a spear that he had to collect before falling the ground.

When his turn came, the groom threw the spear in the air but it dropped in the sea. Without any hesitation, the man dived into the water with the horse, sinking into the waves. With a great surprise, both the groom and the horse came up close to the boat of the Apostles who carried St. James' body to Galicia

The groom was covered of scallop shells from his head to the feet, and the Apostles interpreted this fact as miraculous, inviting the groom boarding on the boat. Legend has it that after speaking with the Apostles either the groom and many of the marriage guests converted to Christianity.

As we have seen, the boat continued its course towards the north entering the Ría de Aurosa. The Apostles landed near the town of Padrón and here they gave burial (not without difficulty) to St. James' body.

From that moment, as I told you, the Concha was given an increasingly growing meaning: at first a simple pilgrimage of homage to the grave of James, now an authentic and unmistakable symbol of faith, friendship and spirituality.

From immemorial time almost all pilgrims travelling to Compostela use to bring a shell with them, attaching it to the backpack.

Let me open a small bracket on my own shell, indeed on my three shells!

When I left for my first Camino, not having obviously the of Santiago shell, I attached to my backpack three small shells my daughter picked up at the seaside. Each of these shells represented a particular thought, and one of my reasons for the Santiago walk. I protected them and kept them as we usually do with our most precious things for the duration of my trip, and even today they are still with me.

On my Camino, like all the pilgrims, I bought my scallop shell (which immediately found place on my backpack) but the three with whom I started my Walking are obviously those to which I attribute the greatest meaning.

Once I reached the beach of Fisterra, I picked up about twenty shells (but unfortunately, not even one scallop, I can swear it!). Back home those shells were my personal gift to the people I have my heart.

Let me close my personal parenthesis and go back to the Santiago shell and its story and function: but, as far as function …

Due to its particular shape, the Concha has not only a symbolic and spiritual function, but also a practical purpose: it was in fact used by pilgrims as a natural container to gather water and drink along streams and rivers.

In short, a symbol that has remained unchanged for centuries and still today it indissolublely identifies the Way of Santiago!

The Mochila: your new home

If you want to fly,

renounce everything that weighs you down.

(Buddha)

An old italian rhyming quotes? Home, <u>sweet home, tiny as you may be</u>, like a palace you're to me. In fact so it is: at home each of us builds, preserves and finds always one's own small world, made of habits, comfort and spaces.

The bedroom, the kitchen, the wardrobe with lots of clothes, the leisure room, and some storage room to keep things almost useless (or those we do not often use).

Well, forget about all this for whole duration of your Camino.

You will have to walk days and days, under the sun and the rain, sometimes it will make a terrible heat and sometimes it will be cold. You will need to sleep, drink, eat, find shelter, get warm when needed, and then of course also have some room for you.

Throughout the journey, your new home will be the Mochila, Spanish word meaning backpack and you will only rely on it and yourself, obviously.

Now, you start understanding how important the choice of the backpack and its contents is, isn'it?

I'm happy for you, but do not worry, in fact I only understood it on my Camino, although thanks to the documents I could studied (in addition to a bit of common good sense and the help of a friend) luckily I started my way properly equipped!

That is why I want to share my experience with you: **Your first Pilgrim's Way to Santiago should be even better than mine.**

Let's go back to the backpack.

As I told you, your home will represent all your world on the way, and it will have to contain everything you need: remember, however, that a backpack (unless you carry it by a specialized company, but we will see it together later) is carried on one's shoulders!!

I know, it's an evident fact, but I'm not making fun of you! Try imagining that you should carry on your shoulders such a weight for an average time of 5 to 6 hours per day: do you have any idea how much it can affect on your fatigue and how much it can not only slow down your walking speed but also how painful it can be?.

One of the things I discovered by preparing my first Santiago Way (and as you know I've always been a pretty lazy person) is that people who for the first time face a long walk tend to overload their shoulders.

Do you know what the problem is? The problem is that a heavy backpack greatly increases fatigue, and especially stresses your back, joints and feet.

Many pilgrims who like me and you deal with the Way for the first time often realize the problem only after a few days of travelling, and unfortunately sometimes it happens that it is really too late to avoid the typical problems of overweight: back pain, inflammation of the joints, feet blisters.

The problem about overweight is so widespread that in many hostels there are spaces in which fatigued pilgrims give their excess objects to those who may need, and even many pilgrims who send home the superfluous.

What about superfluous?. **Thanks to the Camino you'll learn how to do without superfluous stuff, since our only home will be the backpack and we will have to carry it on our shoulders all the time.**

During the preparation of my Path on the website trekking.com, I found this sentence that particularly impressed me: "**If you do not**

bring anything, you will not need anything!".

It is obviously just a hyperbole to focus on the essentials, but it gives you the correct idea, isn'it?.

The first thing you need to know is this: **the perfect backpack should not exceed** (all inclusive) a weight of 10% of your body. Here a few quick examples: a 70kg man should limit the backpack weight tnot over 7kg; a 52kg woman should limit the weight of the backpack just a litlle bit over 5kg.

It seems very simple but actually it is not!.

I've been doing more and more tests. Put and remove, remove and put, a pretty long job.

But a job that you should not absolutely underestimate!.

For each day of your journey, your backpack will be your home and, basically, the container of stuff you can bring with you as well as the only available space for you (including gifts, souvenirs, and any purchases you make on your trip).

You have already realized that it is crucial not only to devote time and attention to the choice of content (things that you will need and can bring with you) but also and above all of the container itself (i.e. ... the backpack!).

How to choose your backpack

Except when I went to school (we talk about the past millennium, alas!) I never owned a backpack, especially one suitable for trekking. That's why I invested a lot of time in choosing the backpack that best suits my purpose.

Capacity:

The first aspect to consider is of course the capacity, in short you have to choose a backpack suitable for carrying what you want to carry with you.

Before speaking about the different types of backpacks depending on the capacity I open a short parenthesis. It seems trivial to say, but be careful: the capacity also affects dimensions; then if you decide to reach your destination with a low-cost airline the size is decisive!.

To reach Vigo, on the Portuguese Path, I chose the most popular low-cost airline in Europe, and in fact, despite being very fussy and rigorous about the size of luggage to carry in the cabin, they did not make me the least problem. The fact that I did good once does not mean that it is (or will be) the rule. Therefore pay attention to the dimensions: excessive measures or weights may lead you to have to pay high extra money!

Let's go back to the backpack capacity:

- 10 liters: the ultralight (and extremely cheap) backpacks available at stores like Decathlon. It's very useful to keep all little things you may need while walking thus avoiding to take off and put back in the main backpack every time.

- 25-35 liters: the size of school backpacks. Ideal for daytime walks or for experienced walkers.

- 40-50 liters: a good weight/capacity compromise, great for the summer period, to be carefully evaluated for a winter walk.

- 50-60 liters: the typical hiking backpack, valid for every season of the year, and certainly the mostly used by pilgrim. I chose a 50 liters one and I found it just perfect, for a 10-day walking.

- Over 60 liters: there are some backpacks that reach 100 liters, and are perfect for those who intend to bring in complex equipment (cookers, tents ...) but honestly I believe that they are just excessive for the Camino. Are there the Albergues or not?

As I told you I chose a 50 liter backpack, a good solution either for size, weight, practicality and load capacity.

Unisex or not?

Another fundamental aspect for choosing the backpack is its genre: **men and women have of course different physical features**, to be taken in due consideration.

It's a question of shoulders (those of women are usually narrower), but also of breast and back. The shoulder straps of the female backpacks are designed so that they do not bother, curl or pain: the distance between the ventral strap and these is in fact designed to better adapt to the body of women.

I have found many discussions on the various forums where many female walkers confirm that the female backpack is much more comfortable than the unisex type.

The backsupport:

A good backsupport is a fundamental aspect to consider when choosing a backpack: its shape must be such as to allow proper weight distribution.

That's why it is essential that the backsupport is adjustable in height!

The reason is simple: it must be able to adapt well to your height and your anatomy

The ventral belt:

The ventral belt is usually one of the most under considered item but the use of which is fundamental!

If well positioned, the waistband allows to relieve fatigue and pain of shoulders and back.

How should **the ventral belt of your backpack be? Simple, it must be generous**.

What I mean is that it must be well padded, it must be solid, almost tough.

It must be large enough to rest on the hips, so to lift the load from the shoulders and instead to load the weight on the pelvis.

Even the chest strap is important since it allows the top of the backpack to remain in the correct position: this is also adjustable to fit the user's body.

Whatever type of backpack you choose is fundamental that it can be perfectly adjustable for your body. Most of the weight, especially for large backpacks, must weigh on the hips: in this way will be the legs, where the strongest muscles of our body reside, to support the weight, without straining too much shoulders and back. In this way our torso remains erect while also ensuring proper breathing.

How to adjust the backpack once you have it on

After loading the backpack, close the compression straps to secure the load inside. At this point wear it, taking care to loosen all the straps of the transport system and position the ventral belt just above your hips. Now start to tension the lower straps of the shoulder straps by increasing the adherence to the back of the backpack, close the pectoral strap just below the clavicle, and act on the load booster belts to form an approx 30° angle.

Reducing the stuff to carry to essential and preparing the backpack in the right way, the load transport is easier.

How to load your backpack:

Of course everyone has one's own habits, even regarding organization of space, so you can choose how to properly load your backpack based on your tastes and your personal habits.

In this section, however, I'm telling you how I organized the content of my **mochila**.

It took several hours to define the contents (we will see it in the next paragraph) as well as the filling order but in the end I can say that I was satisfied.

I started to fill the backpack by placing bulky but not heavy objects on the bottom, such as the sleeping bag, the pillowcase, and the sweatshirt.

Higher on the back I have placed the heaviest objects, such as shoes, beautycase and more. Next to these objects, but separated from my back, I placed the lightest objects: clothes, underwear, towel, etc.

I used the top of the backpack to put all the things I used more often, such as the battery charger, the documents, gadgets, souvenirs bought on the way, and so on.

In the side pockets, the weight of which should always be evenly distributed, I kept at hand all things potentially useful while walking: water bottle, poncho, hat, fruit and snacks.

In short, unless you want to spend hours and hours to do and undo the backpack to look for some object in the meantime disappeared, my advice is to check carefully how to place the objects that you have decided to take with you.

What to put in your backpack:

Like for all the important things, I left deliberately this part as the last of the section dedicated to the backpack.

You've already chosen (or already owned) your backpack now is the time to go to action.

You'll remember that a few pages ago I told you how fundamental it is to concentrate on the essentials, reducing to the utmost the superfluous.

Surely you will be asked how pilgrims had done their Camino through the centuries, when there were no smartphones, shoes and technical equipment, and much of what we use nowadays.

In the past the pilgrims made their way almost without eating and avoiding vices such as smoking, drinking, and try to imagine in what hygienic and health conditions!

Fortunately, times, habits and even technology have changed. The widespread well-being makes each pilgrim face the journey in conditions unthinkable until a few decades ago. The experience of millions of pilgrims and the spread of knowledge makes every outgoing pilgrim aware and especially prepared. Thanks to the technology and the new European Mobile Data Regulation (data and voice) we can use our apps and tools even in the most remote places, just while we are walking.

But remember that the Camino means also sacrifice and renunciation. So pay attention to indispensable stuff and reduce the superfluous.

In this era of hyperconnection, and uncontrolled consumerism, where everything runs so fast and where we do not give ourselves the chance to enjoy anything, you too will discover how I did, the feeling of living with the essential, with the awareness that all you need is ... on your back!

In short, it is time to put into practice what I told you about! I needed several hours to find the perfect equipment and the optimal distribution of my stuff, and this is in my opinion the perfect list of things to put in the backpack. Obviously the list can be improved, so your suggestions will be more than welcome!

- **Clothing:**

  ○ **3 pairs of socks**, of which at least two of the technical type.

  ○ **3 pairs of panties**

  ○ **2 pairs of shorts**

  ○ **1 long trouser**

  ○ **3 short sleeve t-shirts**

  ○ **1 sweater / sweatshirt**

  ○ **1** *Windproof jacket*

  ○ **1 pair of sandals**

- **Accessories:**

  ○ **1 microfibre towel**: it dries quickly, you can use it for every need. They cost little and are very light and practical.

  ○ **1 sleeping bag, or linen bag**: as emergency solution ○ **1 waterproof poncho**: always keep it at hand because weather may change suddenly and you may need it. On the other hand, walking in the rain is a priceless feeling!

  ○ **1 Waterproof Backpack Cover**: You have to protect your backpack as your home because it is, under all respects. It's not fun to find out that because of rain all your clothes and things are drenched!

  ○ **1 water bottle**: I chose a 1.5 liter model. Water weighs, it's true, but for walking you need to keep you hydrated. Often along the way you will encounter drinking water fountains, with abundant, fresh and free water! For me it was a great investment, and a weight that was largely tolerable.

  ○ **1 cap**: it protects you from sun and drizzle!

  ○ **front lamp:** the day I arrived in Santiago with my roommate, we left with large advance before dawn, walking for hours lit only by the stars, and a small torch. It costs little, takes very little space and in case of night walking it can really help preventing path incidents!

- **Hygiene and personal well-being:**

○ **Neutral Marseille soap:** choose the type of soap that can be used for laundry and personal hygiene: a great expedient for saving space and weight.

○ **toothbrush and toothpaste;**

○ **Vaseline**: essential to prevent (or reduce at most) feet blisters. Little cost, you find it anywhere and it is a wonderful ally!

○ **sunscreen cream**: It's true, the weather can be extremely variable, and temperatures mild, but I would not be joking with the sun! Actually, you have to walk for hours and for days so better to avoid sunbathing, isn't?.

○ **medical patches, sterile gauze:** a good assortment is part of the philosophy "you never know which you would need".

○ **bladder patches**: following the precautions I'm going to tell you should minimize the risk of the dreadful blisters, but if it will be the case these patches can really help you. I have chosen non-branded ones: same effectiveness but costing a third!

○ **needle and thread**: desperate problems call for desperate remedies so if serious bladders appear, better to intervene immediately than to suffer, do you agree?

○ **amuchina/chlorine bleach**: a disinfectant can always be necessary

○ **medicinals**: This is obviously an extremely personal and subjective choice, and I would recommend to talk to your medicine doctor. I started with my "emergency" kit: an anti-inflammatory (like aspirin), an antipyretic (like tachipirine) and analgesic (such as Voltaren). Many people also add a stomach disinfectant, or a generic anti-inflammatory drug. Obviously in Spain there are pharmacies and medicines, but I have equipped my basic kit before leaving, so that you can have the minimum indispensable, and do not waste time searching for outlets and products.

○ **bedding products**: the bed bugs were one of my biggest fears, but I never had any problems. Yet, better to go safe!

○ **dietary upplements**: they can be useful if they are part of your habits or necessities.

- **Documents:**

○ identity card and health card;

○ travel documents and tickets

○ **Pilgrim Credentials**: You need it to get access to the available facilities, and get Compostela when you arrive in Santiago.

○ **cash, cash dispenser card or credit cards:** I have not found many cash dispenser, and almost always the add local commissions. Pilgrim's life is low-cost, but get smartly organized.

○ **Mobile phone, battery charger, spare power bank, plug adapter and headset**: sometimes you can not charge the phone for hours, preferably be ready. Sometimes sleeping in certain places will not be easy: headphones can help you not hear dozens of people snore!

○ **Diary and Pen**: ok, with smartphone and social you can tell everything in real time, with lots of photos and videos. But there's no comparison to sit at a coffee table, perhaps with a cerveza and a bocadillo, and write down your thoughts and emotions black on white?

Well, the backpack (indeed, the Mochila) is ready. You too have made dozens and dozens of tests, but in the end you have found your right fit. Now, after managing with the backpack, there is another key element to be chosen properly, as the well-being of your Camino depends upon it. I'm talking about shoes!

Choose the right shoe!

My mama always said you can tell a lot about a person by his shoes, where he's going to, what he does, where he comes from.

(from Forrest Gump movie)

Would you go to work wearing flip-flops? Probably not, unless you work in a swimming pool of course. Would you like to play a soccer match with your friends with a pair of elegant moccasins? I do not believe so. Every occasion requires suitable clothing, but also shoes, and this is also valid for the Camino.

I have already told you how much of the Way you will be walking dirt roads, trails, and in any case ground funds not exactly polished. In short, it's not exactly like doing a stroll in the city center.

Remember that you will walk every day for miles, spending hours with a backpack on your shoulders: the shoes you're going to wear will be an indispensable element for the success of your pilgrimage.

What's the right shoe? Very nice question: the shoe topic has an almost infinite development, along the way I have seen all kinds of them: heavy, lightweight, trekking or running, waterproof or not, of any shape and color (well, it's okay to be a pilgrim, but with a bit of style, Gosh!).

Indeed, the answer is: the perfect shoes are those you feel more suitable for your feets!

Choose the shoes you prefer but the important thing is that they have been already tested: do you remember how your feet feels when wearing new shoes for the first time?

The ideal shoes should have walked at your feet at least a hundred kilometers, so feet and shoes will be used to each other and you just have to worry about taking one step after another! **Do not choose a shoe that is of the "right" size**: as you can imagine walking for hours will cause your feet to swell, so choose a one or half-foot size over the usual ones. In the traits where height difference occurs (ascents / descents) a larger shoe allows you to reduce the rubbing of your fingers and nails against the side of the shoe. Many say that between the foot and the side of the shoe you should be able to insert a finger. The shoe you'll use should be comfortable: walking with a heavy shoe can become a torture, so choose a shoe that fits your foot well, which is not excessively heavy and of course it must be robust!

When I had to choose my shoe I opted for a hiking shoe, low model since I almost never get to the mountain (at least ... until now!) and waterproof. In short, I tried to choose a ductile shoe, which could be used in different conditions and moments. I thought in fact that a high summer shoe might be too heavy and tiring for the foot but at the same time that a waterproof shoe could be a good help in the event of rain or crossing streams or else.

In fact, several thinkings are against waterproof shoes for summertime as they are heavier, but recommend breathable shoes.

How to Avoid Feet Blisters

I am a moderately courageous person, I have a pretty strong adaptation spirit, and yet there are things I can not bear! One of these is the pain.

I try to use the medicines only when I absolutely can not avoid them and do everything to prevent, with the hope of being able to avoid post treatement.

This is to tell you that when I began to get informed about organizing my Camino I immediately knew about this plague that affects tens of thousands of pilgrims: the blisters at the feet!

Since in my former life the only sport I was concerned with was to give the results of the matches during my radio program, you may understand with what horror I found that walking could have slaughtered my feet! Never be!.

As you know, the blisters are lesions that appear on the skin of the feet: the skin swells and fills with fluid. Ok is not the end of the world, it is not a serious problem if you are at home and you have to walk a little, but along the Way it can become a real torture: blisters can cause pain, burns and in many cases can also make difficult an elementary activity such as simple walking. Imagine if you have to walk for tens of miles every day, with a heavy backpack on your shoulders!

Feet blisters are often caused by pressures and chafing of the foot on socks and shoes. Socks and shoes too tight, low quality, uncomfortable or with a particular shape represent a potential danger; the risk may increase in summertime due to high temperatures and humidity.

Of course, even long walks wearing hiking booties, perhaps on dirt roads or trails, are among the possible causes of blisters.

You have already understood: the Camino may the bes tool for you to get signed up at the Great World Championship of Painful Feet. Do you wanna win it? I guess not!.

I did not, nor wished to enroll myself. The good thing is that for the whole length of my Camino I was able to avoid any bladder: I just adopted some small "tricks" and I managed to treat my feet well! No bladder, no pain but just obviously the fatigue of tens of miles with backpack on shoulders.

The first way to avoid the blisters is **to choose a shoe that fits your foot**: choose with care the couple of shoes that you will use along your Way, maybe following the advice of the chapter "Choose the right shoe". The shoes are the key for the well-being of your feet, they can represent the difference between a beautiful and carefree trip and a valley of tears!

Another basic element for the health of your foot is the **sock**. Avoid normal socks, focus your choice on seamless, breathable socks, conceived for long walkings. You'll find of all kinds and, not least, of all prices.

In all my purchases I always try to find the best quality/price ratio, because I realized that quite often you can find top quality products spending a little less, and since the Camino definitely does not need designer clothing, if you dedicate some time to choosing the right equipment but at an appropriate price it can contribute to the delight of your journey.

Let's think about this: you've chosen the shoes and the socks that fit your feet. Every day you protect your feet with these and walk for 20/30 kms carrying on them not only your body but also a weight of at least 7 to 8 kgs. What do you think of doing when you reach your destination?, after taking a shower and a snack, I mean.

Well, I used to take off my booties and socks as soon as I could just on my arrival and left my feet free to breathe until the next morning. That's why I took a pair of sandals with me (remember, I advised you to do the same) to allow the feet to rest and to breathe. If you the release your feet and enjoy a shower, your lower extremities will largely breathe … as well as your adventure fellows will do!.

Allow your feet to breathe as soon as possible, but also keep your body hydrated. Of course, you already know it, but always remember it: keeping our body constantly and rightly hydrated is an essential condition at any time in our life. Mostly important during the Camino; In Galicia, for example, the wind and the mild climate might not make you feel the need to drink, but do a favor for your body and hydrate it. Your feet will be happy too!

I am a person who usually drinks a lot: at least two liters of water a day, every day. Well, on my way I have maintained and increased this habit: I have always drank at least two liters of water per day while walking, and of course also during the rest of the day. Hydrated body means hydrated feet and this results in well-being!.

Now, last but not least, I'm telling you my personal cure-all to prevent feet blisters during my Santiago walking. It's a remedy, rather a preventive method, which I discovered by documenting me on the sites dedicated to running, trekking and of course the Way.

Every morning before you leave, **spread plenty vaseline on your feet**. Before leaving for my journey I bought two small tubes (to comply with flight restrictions on liquids), for the amount of 3€, my summer best paid money!

By greasing your feet with vaseline you will considerably reduce the friction of the skin against socks and shoes, so you can greatly reduce the risk of blisters. For example, I did not even have one, but this is obviously just my experience.

What I can tell you is that vaseline is super cheap, and it's easy to use: just take the tube and spread it over your whole foot, plant and fingers in a particular way. This will reduce friction and soften your feet further!.

I repeat, this is just my experience but I can assure you that the hypothesis of having my feet tortured was a nightmare for me. With these simple arrangements I managed to have no problem at all!.

Good luck to you and when you come back, please, let me know about your experience!.

S.O.S Backpack!

My backpack is not just loaded with stuff and food: inside I have my manners, my affections, my memories, my character, my solitude.

Up the mountains I do not bring the best of myself: I carry myself, for good and for bad.

(Renato Casarotto)

You've made all the right choices: backpack, shoes, bladder cream, workout and everything else. So far everything is fine.

Obviously, the wish is that all pilgrims can make their journey without problems, but especially for those who choose the longest and most difficult routes some little unexpected inconvenients are possible: pains, tendinitis, small accidents may require periods of rest or more simply a few days of less demanding walk.

As you could learn, the Camino consists in a network of well-organized roads, trails and dirt roads, fundamentally safe, very frequented and provided with every kind of service.

There are several companies that offer pilgrims a luggage shift service (and if necessary for the pilgrims themselves) that allows you to send your backpack from one Albergue to the other.

These services are not present on all the routes of the Camino, so it is good to organize yourself in time and to know about their availability along the way you decide to go.

I have met several pilgrims who, because of hardly bearable pains, have made the most wisdom choice to continue the walk without backpack. I think there is nothing wrong or contrary to the spirit of the Way: such experience requires a spirit of adaptation and sacrifice but within a certain limit, do you agree with me?.

The cost varies according to the route your luggage will make and other factors. The average cost per stage is about 7 €.

In each accommodation you will find the numbers of the various services and you can agree on the conditions and prices of the transport. Usually the albergue will also provide you with an envelope, to be completed with your phone number, destination and albergue name, to be attached on your backpack.

Usually the backpack is picked up by 8 am and delivered in the early afternoon: almost always when you reach the hotel your backpack will be there, rest and waiting for you.

In the Resources section, you will find a list of the best known companies that do this service.

Sleeping on the Camino

A good laugh and a long sleep are the best care in the doctor's book.

(Irish Saying)

However tiring and sometimes exhausting, the Camino can grant not only unique emotions, but also a perfect organization, tested by centuries and centuries of incessant pilgrimages.

You will worry about weather (but if you leave well equipped, even weather will not be a big obstacle), be afraid of bugs or feet blisters, but there are some aspects you will never have to worry about, and I'm talking about two really essential ones: eating and sleeping.

In this chapter, in particular, I will talk about the many possibilities you will find for refreshment after a long day of walking along your path.

You will have a great network of hospitality options: from private homes, or parish and communal hostels, to the very classic Albergues and Hostal I will talk about in this chapter of my book.

Concerning private homes and accommodations: On my book site you will receive 25 € credit on your next trip with Airbnb, go here: https://goo.gl/2Zj2bc. If you have never used Airbnb this is a great opportunity to start enjoying the hospitality of really unique places.

Several pilgrims also spent one or more nights (of course in the summer months, and with good weather) under the stars, after finding a comfortable and safe clearing. Honestly, even though I suppose it could be a wonderful experience, I avoided it, for safety reasons (we'll talk about safety later on), and because bringing a tent with you (though lightweight) represents a significant weight increase, unless you really sleep only in your sleeping bag. We therefore know better about the typical reception facilities that you will find anywhere along your Camino.

The Albergues

Albergue is the Spanish equivalent of hostels, therefore, rather spartan and quite cheap structures that allow pilgrims to find hospitality for the night. These structures are almost always managed by private people, or municipalities, religious organizations, or associations of Camino friends. There are also facilities managed by Italian authorities, such as the Confraternity of St. James.

You will find the Albergues very easily on the main routes (the French and the Portuguese are really well equipped from this point of view), well-distributed on the route and present at every stage. This feature will allow you to better organize the stages of your journey.

Traditionally, the Albergues welcome pilgrims for one night only, unless there are special conditions (illness, accident, unforeseen inconveniences). On the other hand, one of the characteristics of the Way is the day-to-day trip, where one night you sleep in a place, and the night after ... anywhere else.

At the Albergues you can sleep by spending very little, although of course the rates are different from one structure to another: as to my experience I never spent more than 8-15 € per night. Then consider that to honor the spirit of the Camino there are structures that accept only a donation, thus allowing those who do not have sufficient means to sleep even for free.

The rule is that you sleep in common rooms, therefore men and women, friends and not. There are no "double bed" solutions but only single beds. Some Albergues, especially private ones, have started to offer even more comfortable and private rooms, obviously with an additional cost.

Another fundamental rule of the Albergues: all the pilgrims presenting the Credential are welcomed, with priority to those who travel on foot and then to cyclists, of course depending on the availability of beds and the time of arrival.

When you are in your Albergue do not forget to ask the Hospitarelos (the structure manager) to stamp the *sello* (stamp) on your Credential. It is necessary to attest your passage theer as well as personal remembrance!

Reservations: this is a delicate key! In fact, the Albergues do not require booking, and often they do not even allow it. Almost everywhere the rule is "those who first come first served": I do not think there is any need for explanation, isn'it?.

Remember that even in the Albergues (almost always private ones) where reservations are accepted, they are valid until a certain time. Usually it works like this: they hold the reservation until 16 pm, so if you are present in time you're welcome, but if you get late and in the meantime someone else has passed, you have a problem to solve.

I have seen many hostels open not before and this makes sense: pilgrims leave early in the morning and that is the time when most arrives at their destination!

However, since every Albergue has its own rules, I strongly recommend that if you decide to book, to inform you well of the rules of the reservation: after a day of Cammino I imagine you will be rather tired, so better not facing any surprises, do you agree?.

It is also true that the spirit of the Camino and the organization of the Albergues mean that wherever you find the sign "full", they almost always are able to assist you some way.

About the timetables: Hostels are generally open between 3:30 pm and 6 pm up to 10 am the morning after. The closing time is used by the operators for cleaning operations. This, however, means another thing: when you arrive you will find the newly clean toiletries. I suggest you take advantage of it as soon as possible. My personal experience taught me that almost never are cleansed until the next day, and let you imagine what it's like to have a horde of incoming pilgrims after a long day on the Path!. Let's simply say, "who first comes, better ...." (fill the dots with what comes to your mind).

What will you find in the Albergues?

As I said, the albergues offer a very basic accommodation, suitable for spending a night comfortably, safely and protected. There are structures of all kinds, old and new, public or private, with different levels of cleanliness, comfort, services and of course price (from 6/10 € to 15/18 €).

Remember that dormitories are commonplace, as well as the toilets.

Basically all the albergues provide pilgrims with these services:

• **A bed**: it's almost always bunk beds in dorms of varying sizes, but I have also seen even more minimalistic accommodations with mattresses resting on the floor or emergency camp beds. Apart from the bed, other services are offered at the discretion of the property: sometimes you will find only the bed, sometimes the linen and / or the blanket, in some cases even towels. Since every albergue has actually its service features better to start with one's own sleeping bag in the backpack and (at least) the cover for the pillow.

• **Showers and bathrooms** almost always with hot water and toilet paper. I dare give you some important tips: remember to take the soap (better if Marseille as you can use it for personal hygiene but also for laundry), a roll of toilet paper and plastic slippers!!.

• **Laundry**: though I've always been used to be as independent as possible I learned to do laundry only during my Camino!!. Think, I had to write this book to convince my mother that I really started to wash my clothes! Leaving aside my personal stories, in the Albergues you'll almost always find spaces dedicated to laundry: simple washbasins where you can wash your stuff and lay them to dry; or rooms equipped with lavadora and secadora (washing machine and dryer), obviously in this case you'll pay and extra cost. Consider that the full service costs between 6 and 8 euros: if you can arrange with other pilgrims to do laundry, then using lavadora and secadora can be a good idea since you will share the costs!.

• **Kitchen**: Many Albergues have a common room for preserving and preparing meals; they are often equipped with cooker or stove, pots and tableware. Many pilgrims make purchases in the tiendas (shops) or in supermarkets in the village, and then cook in the hostel. Ever since, meals are one of the first moments of conviviality and sociality, a great way to open up to other people and to know them, so you may often attend (or participate) at dinners organized by pilgrims just known. One evening, in a hostel in Fisterra, I tried to teach a group of Dutch pilgrims how to enjoy ravioli, but when I realised that they wanted to season them with the Ketchup ... I thought it was best to run away!.

• **Breakfast** (desayuno) and dinner. There are those who prefer to go straight ahead and stop in a bar along the way; or someone uses the kitchen to arrange breakfast in autonomy, or those who prefer to rely on the Hospitaleros. In many Albergues it is possible to have breakfast (and maybe even a collective dinner) with a few euros: brioches, café con leche, homemade cakes and whatever the facility makes available.

• **Wi-fi**: available in many facilities, almost always free of charge. However, remember to check the conditions of your phone operator: after the abolition of European roaming, the use your connection is no longer expensive as in the past!.

• **Infirmary**: small cabinet equipped with commonly used medications for problems such as blisters, slight wounds etc. The hospitaleros also have telephone numbers for medical assistance or ambulance assistance.

• **Relax areas** where you can take a break at the end of the journey, in the sun or shade, sitting on a comfortable chair, a bench, a low wall or lying on the lawn, drinking a cool beer, writing the notes of the day, studying the stage for tomorrow or chatting with other pilgrims.

Tips for sleeping in dorms

If like me you've never slept before now in a hostel (or Albergue) then the following tips may be useful:

• **Get informed**: every albergue has its services, its rules, its features and provides a different hospitality, avoids surprises and get well informed!

- **Community**: bathrooms, kitchens and dormitories are all common spaces to be shared with other guests, get organized accordingly!

- **Prudence**: trust is good, not trust it better! Since you sleep with perfect strangers and you do not know their intentions, do not leave valuables in the room. Albergues will not be held liable unless you decide to use the security boxes (payable).

- **Respect**: The first night I spent in the dormitory, those several funny guys came in at three o'clock at night howling like wolves. In that moment, my good intentions as pilgrim would gladly leave room for the version of myself with Katana. In the dormitory, the pilgrims want to rest, therefore, avoiding night-time jokes, high-volume music, exaggerated disorder, and everything that does not fall within the rules of civil life. Of course, though I know you'll respect these trivial rules, you may encounter annoying roommate sooner or later. Breathe, get armed with calm and patience and bear, and if you just do not ... kindly ask to respect the silence.

- **Noise**: Many pilgrims stand up before dawn, then there are those who go to the bathroom at night or make noises of any kind. I honestly believe that after the second / third day of your Camino you will fall asleep as a poppy after pulling his milk, but if you have a light sleep use ear plugs and sleeping mask. If you're used to get asleep with music, uou're OK!!.

- **Socialize**: Albergues pilgrims, especially the solitary ones, love to make acquaintances. Open your heart to your roommates: two chats before turning off the light, a dinner together will be unforgettable experiences!.

- **Ask**: sleeping in an albergue does not mean giving up your own habits or necessities. If you have any special needs, ask the staff, you will always find nice people who will listen to you.

- **Relax**: You are doing a great experience, you are knowing new people, and you are also saving money. Is not this the time to enjoy all this?.

The Hostel

Here a riddle for you: if the spagnish word Albergue (which in italian means hotel) refers to hostel, what do you think a "Hostel" is?.

Bravo! You guessed it: it's the hotel! For language lovers, these two words (hostel and albergue, but also for butter/burro and so many others) are false friends, that is   with a different meaning!.

In short: if you are looking for a hostel you have to find an Albergue, while looking for a hotel you need to find a Hostel. Simple!.

Obviously the Hostels offer different services and levels of comfort from the Albergues: single, double, triple or quadruple rooms with almost always private bathroom and everything you need.

Prices for intermediate facilities are extremely competitive: from 18 euros for a 2-star, to 42 euros for a four-star hostel. Almost always breakfast is a separate cost, and almost always these rates are valid only for pilgrims.

The day I arrived in Pontevedra with my new travel companions, for example, after trying in vain for a couple of albergues we opted for this solution: we entered the first Hostel met on the road, we contracted a bit and we could enjoy (after 3 nights in albergue) the first night in a real bed and the first private shower! You can not understand our enjoyment!!.

In short: in case you find all the albergues full up, or if you wish for a more comfortable night, you can easily use a Hostel!

Unlike the Albergues virtually all Hostels accept bookings so it's really easy to use the major websites to book your accommodation without any anxiety and no trouble connected to your arrival time.

If you do not like spartan accommodations, you can always decide to always sleep in Hostels. You can, of course, leave your Country with all the bookings already fixed, or you can book it from day to day, with the opportunity to change your route and your walkthrough chart.

Do not think about what others are doing, you do not have to prove anything to anyone (if not to yourself) so arrange your Camino in the way that most suits your tastes and needs!.

Your Camino should be like you: unique!.

What to eat along the Camino?

"I'll definitely lose weight," or "I take advantage of this for my diet", are just some of the phrases (accompanied by all the other possible variants) that I have said and I've heard from practically all the pilgrims I met on my way.

The intent is more than noble and logical: walking and striving mean embracing the original spirit of the pilgrimage (which included half fasting conditions) and being essential even in nourishment.

The intent is good, at least until you make the first (and then the second, the third and all the others) meeting with the Spanish, and Galician cuisine.

In the next chapter, we will talk about slimming, but in the meantime we think of the good things you will encounter along the Way.

Spanish cuisine in general, and Galician in particular, is a cuisine rich in tradition and flavors, able to satisfy the most diverse palates but of course one of the great classics of the Way is the "pilgrim menu", offered in thousands of facilities (bars, restaurants, tabernas etc) in as many variants, both for lunch and dinner.

The price is always quite small and ranges between 8 and 12 euros per person. The pilgrim (or "dia") menu represents a good meal both in terms of quality and quantity. On average the price includes:

- A first dish: very seldom with pasta (anyway, being Italian, I would avoid it and wait for the return home) more often a soup (sopa), a salad with the inevitable tomatoes (tomates) or tuna (atún), or spanish salami (chorizo, jamon).

• A second dish with meat or fish. The lomo (pork loin) served on the plancha (plate), asado (roast) or guisado (stew), as well as of course the chicken, other cuts of pork or calf and the cod (which is an Atlantic fish, merluza).

- Side dish: potatoes in all variants, beans (alubias), green beans (judías verdes).

- Dessert: Santiago cake, ice cream (helado), arroz con leche (rice with milk), flan (pudding).

Pay attention to bottled mineral water asit's always quite expensive. I usually asked for source water or a very good local beer (cerveza) either a bottle or in glass.

Sometimes the pilgrim's menu is a good solution, but personally after a couple of times I said stop!.

Local cuisine is full of wonderful and varied flavors, so why not widen the choice?. Galicia offers authentic delicacies, spending always a small amount of money, provided you avoid the traps for tourists or starred restaurants (yes, there are also a lot of great restaurants in this wonderful land!).

So here is a short list of delicious foods that you absolutely have to taste on the different stages of your Camino (or during the walk, at lunch):

- **Octopus** (pulpo): the fleshy and excellent polyps of the Atlantic. In Galicia the octopus is offered everywhere, especially in the *pulperies,* typical premises where this dish is offered in infinite and spectacular variations!. Do not miss the great local specialty: the "pulpo a gallega" (or 'a feira'), boiled, cut into pieces and seasoned with oil, salt and paprika, sometimes accompanied with potatoes. I will never forget the first time I ate this dish in a small restaurant overlooking the Poio beach, with a frozen cerveza! But beware of the octopus: it makes addiction!!.

- **Crustaceans**: They are mussels, clams, cannoliers, oysters, crabs, grannies or scallops (the concha shell symbol of Santiago), and you will find them always and everywhere fresh and very good. Galicia is a land (or rather sea) of crustaceans and shellfish farming, which from here leave to be sold in much of Europe. One of the traditions when arriving in Santiago is for example to celebrate the end of the Camino with a rich dinner of crustaceans. As if it were not enough on Wednesdays at the market in Santiago you can buy fresh molluscs and crustaceans from fishmongers and ask to cook them at the moment. The expense is about 4 euros per head.

• **Pimiento de Padron**: other addictive substance! They are the green, small, tasty peppers of Galicia (identified by the Controlled Origin Denomination). Stir-fried and salted on the surface they are a very tasty and traditional dish. I keep dreaming about them every night: do not miss!

• **Empanada gallega**: yes, beyond the tortilla there is more, and this is empanada. It is served as a free pincho with a cane of cerveza or if you decide to have it as a complete meal know that it is a very good salty cake, square shaped, filled with tuna, peppers, olives, onions or meat.

• **Lacon Gallego**: If the Galician coast is the kingdom of fish and crustaceans, the inland offers salami and I can say that the ones I tasted are really good. Lacon is the raw ham typical of these areas: it melts in your mouth and is really sweet. If you love Parma or San Daniele ham, you will also love Lacon!.

• **Percebes**: Still fish, or better seafood. The look is not particularly inviting, but just try it out to enjoy an authentic delight!

I talked about pilgrim's menu and local specialties for lunch and dinner but I have not referred anything about one of the main meals of the day: breakfast.

Have you ever heard that saying "Take breakfast as a king, lunch as a prince, dinner as a poor"?. Actually, breakfast should be the main meal of the day, and should normally give us between 15 and 20% of the calories we will use during the day.

According to some studies, a good breakfast is of fundamental importance in preventing some of the problems that can affect our body: it reduces the possibility of developing diabetes mellitus, experiencing cardiovascular problems, overweight, obesity and stress.

It does not end here: the level of blood sugar on awakening is low, and the consequence is that without proper glucose intake our body system will be subjected to a greater sense of hunger. Avoiding breakfast or not taking an appropriate one requires frequent snacks, or excess lunches (resulting in digestive difficulties and drowsiness) and maybe excess dinners. The result is we cannot burn excess calories and make us find the next morning without appetite.

In short, a good breakfast is the best way to deal not only with the Santiago Way but every day of our lives, whether or not working.

Keep in mind that the pilgrim's day begins quite early (very often between 5 and 7 am). I almost always had breakfast in the hostel. Where the breakfast service was not offered, I usually bought some food in one of the many grocery stores or markets found along the way.

The Spanish breakfast is very similar to the Italian one, so for this meal (desayuno) in the albergues or bars you can usually find: cafè con leche (coffee with milk), cortado de leche o de cafè (milk or coffee with milk), café corto (express coffee), muffins or similar, tostada (toasted bread) with tomates (tomatoes) or mantequilla y marmelada (butter and jam), or aceite (oil), churros (fritters), confectionery pastries.

Pat attention to bars! If you are used to having breakfast early in the bar close your home, remember that the Spanish rhythms are far different as they open a few hours later. I can tell you that I hardly encountered bars open before 9am! If you do not want to have dangerous mirage of brioches or sandwiches, get organized in time!.

One of the unmissable moments of my day along my Camino was the "cerveza break". From my point of view a fresh beer (in bottle or "*cana*") is a wonderful moment to exchange two chats with other pilgrims or with local people. The local beer is light but tasty, really good!.

Cerveza is almost always served with the "pincho", a snack of variable size and type: from small bocadillo (sandwich) with ham, or small portions of tortillas or so on. The only limit is the chef's fantasy.

One thing that surprised me in all my Cerveza breaks was the expense: never more than 1.80 € for a good beer and a pinch. Not bad, isn'it?.

In any case, you have a wide and maybe difficult choice among tortillas, bocadillos and the best of galician cuisine even for a simple snack.

I close this chapter with some simple tips for feeding on the Path, of course these are general advice that you will have to evaluate personally.

• Breakfast: The ideal would be to choose foods containing carbohydrates and sugars with little sucrose and very fructose. Biscuit bread, jam, honey, coffee with biscuits and fruit.

• Morning snack: carbohydrates (bread, crackers, biscuits) and fruit (no sugar or chocolate).

• Dinner: red or white meat, fish, cheeses, vegetables, bread, wine, fruit.

• Drink a lot of water, regardless of whether or not you sweat; always keep hydrated as it helps to walk with greater well-being, then if the temperatures are high, water, fruits and supplements are indispensable.

Does The Camino help Slimming?

In truth, this chapter is born thanks to Google. In the course of my research before to writing this book, the search engine suggested this sentence, and I must say that it excited my interest quite a lot!.

I have never been (and when I say never I really mean NEVER) a slim person, indeed I have always been rather, let me say, soft.

When I decided to go on my Camino, I also started training in order to be physically ready to support an effort I was not used to. Obviously, I immediately thought of the inevitable side effect that a workout leads to, therefore, the possibility of losing weight.

Speaking with the new friends met on the Path and with many other pilgrims, I realized that Google was right: there are many people who consider the Way experience an opportunity to get into dieting thanks to walking, thus slimming.

But the question remains: can you lose weight?.

In theory it is possible, whilst very difficult in practice. In the blog **thewalkingmed** (you'll find the link in the resource section) Irene Campagna explains why.

Obviously the duration of the pilgrimage, distance traveled, weight carried on, walking speed and physical fitness should heavily affect the final results. Theoretically such a physical effort as intense and long distance as that of walking the Camino should make you actually lose weight, isn'it?

Think about what happens on the average day of a pilgrim: every day you walk about 25 km with a weight of about 10 kg on your shoulders. You walk not too fast (say about 4.5 / 5km / h) but the weight and the differences in elevation make us consume many calories anyway.

Walking for about 6 hours we can estimate approx 3000 and 3600 calories consumption, which are to be added to those we need for the "normal administration" of our daily living, so between 1500 and 2500 calories.

In short, during the days of the Camino we certainly have an important caloric needs, but do not forget that as many calories we will burn, we will probably take on as much. As Irene says, "the greater energy consumption is likely to be balanced by a greater caloric intake; we spend more energy and compensate it by eating even more".

And indeed for me it was just like this: I always had a good breakfast to prepare my day for the best, then got the lunch, some snack reinforce here and there (maybe the classic cerveza with bocadillo) and to complete my day the classic dinner of the pilgrim.

In short, the burning of energy, fatigue, but also the tasty Spanish cuisine have caused the calories intake and consumption to be nearly equivalent!.

As to me I did not not lose weight thanks to the Camino, but I got a good consolation reward or comfort: the long, tiring day-to-day walks have helped increasing my muscle mass (heavier) to the disadvantage of the fat mass (paradoxically lighter). In short, the weight remained the same, but I got more tonic!.

I'd say that anyway it's a good result, right?.

Pilgrim's (health) Problems

A marketing expert recommended me not to include this chapter in my book: he argues that I should emphasize the positive aspects of the Way, and not the inevitable side issues, especially those related to health!

How you may understand I do not agree! I invest myself totally in the things I do or say, and I try to be absolutely honest. It is that life is made of white and black, of too few moments of happiness and (often too many) moments of difficulty.

For these reasons, I think that you must be prepared to know the possible problems you may encounter along your Camino.

In the next chapters I will also talk about two authentic nightmares of pilgrims: bed bugs and blisters, but now I would like to talk to you about the health problems that pilgrims may often encounter on the Path.

Once again I recommend to get documented with your medicine doctor, as I'm not, to get these issues out.

Meanwhile, however, let's see what are the most common problems a pilgrim may encounter.

- **Bladder and inflammation**: In our special ranking of possible pilgrimage problems, these are always in highest position, thus deserving a separate chapter!

- **Muscle pain and contractures**: training and correct posture (backpack included), as well as exercises of heating before starting a new stage and a walk proportionate to one's pace and without forcing can help reduce the risk. If, despite the cautions, any such pains occur, it is necessary to let the affected area rest and eventually assume painkillers.

- **Tendinitis and distortion**: even in this case rest is essential, then you can apply ice (helps to decrease the swelling); you may also need an analgesic-anti-inflammatory to relieve the pain. The main advice is, however, to seek appropriate medical care! Do not make the hero!

• **Sunburns**: Walking in the sun may be overwhelming as well as cause sunburns. Indispensable, therefore, always have a hat, sunglasses and sun protection with a factor of 30 or higher. Do not underestimate Spain sun, even in those areas where the wind prevent from feeling the heat (but the sun does not miss). In case of sunburns it is important to wash the area with cold water without rubbing and applying abundant moisturizer cream. When necessary, assume an analgesic and look for health care doctor (especially in case of large bubbles or sunburn is very extensive).

• **Dehydration**: drink, drink and again drink much water. Keep constantly hydrated according to your needs and remember that not sweating does not mean not to lose liquids, indeed! Remember that wind and other elements may prevent you to feel thirsty, but your body needs water! If possible, avoid walking in the hottest hours of the day and (I repeat) drink plenty of water. In case of severe tiredness and dry mouth, be careful: rest and in case of loss of consciousness or mental confusion, go to the nearest Health Center (Centro de Salud). Since you will find thousands of fountains on your Camino with fresh, free and potable water, always keep your water bottle full!

• **Insect stings**: unfortunately for the pilgrims all insects that populate forests and countryside never go on holiday. In the event of a sting, wash the affected area without rubbing and apply an anti-itch cream. Bring with you an anti-insect cream and avoid any scent that attract them (may I remember you that evening society life is virtually nonexistent along the Camino!).

• **Gastroenteritis**: you should be able to avoid this problem if you drink potable or bottled water, wash well with fruits and vegetables, keep good personal hygiene and avoid eating foods that degrade at room temperature. But should it be the case, it manifests itself with nausea, vomiting, abdominal pain and diarrhea. In some cases there is also fever and a general feeling of illness. Should you have such a problem go to the Health Center (especially in case of vomiting), rest and do not swallow anything during the next 24 to 30 hours. But get hydrated!

• **Mycosis**: always wear rubber sandals when taking a shower and carefully dry your feet; take high care of your personal hygiene. Then apply a specific product if needed. The right attention will avoid unpleasant surprises!.

In the chapter dedicated to the backpack I also describe what you should bring with you, but remember that the Camino begins and ends every day in villages or cities where there is a chemist's store and will also be on your way along the route you'll be passing by as well as villages. We are still in Europe, about whose civilization we must not absolutely have no doubt.

As to me, I have always open a travel insurance, one of those policies that guarantees you a whole set of covers in case of any kind of trouble (from luggage loss to anything else you may think of).

It is an investment that I make every time: just when we are in our environment, small or big accidents can happen, but if something happens to us when we are abroad, how to face it?.

I like to sleep quietly, and I prefer to know that, whatever happens to me, I have an insurance cover that allows me to face the trouble serenely.

Am I too cautious? Maybe it is, but I feel safer!

Remember also that we are in Spain, a country inside the European Community, that means that for the citizens belonging to it there are agreements that guarantee the possibility of receiving assistance.

I invite you to get informed about how the necessary conditions in case of need, but in the meantime I will provide you with the information available on the website Spain.info for healthcare (updated September 2017).

"By submitting the European Health Insurance Card (HEIC), you will

receive assistance from a family doctor at health centers or at home if you are unable to move. If you need a specialist or hospital admission, your doctor will provide you with the corresponding certificate (or request). Hospitals are provided with emergency services.

In any case you need to be in possession of the European Health Card (EHIC).

The European Health Insurance Card will entitle you to receive the same healthcare benefits as Spanish citizens are required for a temporary stay. The validity period is indicated on the same Card, which can be used in all countries of the European Union, including Switzerland, Norway, Iceland and Liechtenstein.

Private Spanish doctors and hospitals do not accept the European Health Card. If you want to receive medical assistance from private services, you will have to either bear the costs yourself or make a health insurance cover for them. "

If necessary the main number for assistance is the **free 112** phone number. This number is valid throughout the Spanish territory. Obviously the operators will answer you in Spanish language and, in the tourist areas, may speak in English, French and German.

The Bugbear of the Camino: the Bed Bugs

Before leaving on my Camino, bed bugs were a real scarecrow for me as I read about really bad situations. Therefore I arranged for an authentic task force anti-parasitic products.

Thanks to my lucky star, I did not meet any problem, and all my sprays came back home and still sealed!

Nevertheless, it is better to deal with this (if any) problem in advance, by getting informed about it, and also how to defeat the terrible bed bugs.

These insects belong to the Cimicidae family, they feed on human and animal blood, mainly affecting areas without hair: legs, arms, and face.

Bed bugs do not fly, but they move on walls and ceilings, from which they drop to pinch their victims, identified by heat, moisture and carbon dioxide released by the body.

They predominantly sting at night during the deeper phase of sleep and skin blush appears in correspondence of the sting a few minutes or few hours later and lasts from one to three weeks. Obviously the effects are different depending on the individual immune response.

The first thing they do is inject saliva, whose anesthetic and anticoagulant function lasts about four hours, after which they suck the blood of their victim. Often the result of their puncture is an annoying and painful skin rash. It is true that they do not transmit viruses or bacteria or else, but since the effect is painful, better avoiding avoid ii. Bed bug stings are similar (and sometimes confusing) to those of mosquitoes, but more annoying and painful, to the point of being infected if they are scratched. Better then resist from scratching or apply some suitable cream!.

Now that you know what they are, find out where they are and, more importantly, how to deal with them.

Obviously like all insects bed bugs prefer dusty and dirty places (hostels and hotels included), however the equation dirt = bug bedding is incorrect. The main vehicle of infestation is man: the passage through woods and meadows can make the pilgrim become bed bugs carrier, and at that point it is easy to imagine what can happen when you get to the hotel.

This is just to say that even the cleanest place can be infested, but there are some solutions to prevent and deal with the problem. To prevent bed bugs:

• Before occupying the bed, look around carefully, especially the mattress and the pillow, which are the favorite places for bedbugs, and of course even floors, walls and furniture.

• Do not put backpack and clothes in dirty places.

• Do you have sleeping bag and cushion cover? Use them!

• Provide with proper spray products and if you notice dirt and degradation in hostel or guests, make a preventive disinfestation!

If you find the bed bugs, immediately inform the hospitalero, so he can proceed with the fumigation disinfestation. Never act if nothing happened: it is true that the next morning we will leave, but new pilgrims will arrive. So do not become accomplice of the contagion.

In the case of a bite the first thing to avoid is scratching: skin lesions can get infected and worsen the situation, rather clean the area of the puncture with water and soap and apply any oily or soothing cream. In case of severe itching, numerous bites or special reactions, seek immediate for medical care.

It is necessary to proceed as quickly as possible to the disinfestation of the backpack and the clothes, washing all the fabrics (backpack, clothes, sleeping bag …) at temperatures above 50°C for a suitable long time (the most experienced say at least 7 minutes).

For many people the solution is to put everything in a black plastic bag to leave in the sun: the temperatures that develop do a real massacre of these parasites!

Sincerely, I did not rely at all on the reports found on Facebook about the presence of bugs in an albergue rather than another: their presence is not synonymous with dirt or carelessness, and now that rumor spells disinfection has already been made.

In any case, as long as the bed bugs are quite disgusting and annoying, remember that a careful look at the mattress and bed will allow you to discover them and decide what to do.

The Hórreos

If you're thinking about biscuits, you will be disappointed: the Hórreos have nothing to do with the famous chocolate snacks.

Although not exactly edible, in fact, hòrreos still have a strong correlation with food, albeit indirectly.

The Horreos are granaries, which were used as warehouses for campaign products, and to store foodstuffs. You will find them in rural areas, almost always next to the owners' houses. Unfortunately, with the gradual abandonment of the countryside, with the advent of agricultural mechanization and with new technologies for the preservation of food and products, the use of the Horreos has been drastically reduced, to the extent that many are abandoned or kept as elements of street furniture.

However the Horreos are extremely popular in the countryside of Asturias and Galicia, highly characteristic of the landscape you will encounter on the Camino.

You will find all types, shapes, sizes and materials, some are in a state of neglect, others will look new, or at least just restored. Their feature also depends on the area they are in, and they were considered as a status symbol: materials, dimensions and shape reflected the wealth and social status of the owner.

The structure of the Horreos is strongly affected by the area in which they are made: the Horreos present in Asturias, for example, have square planes with generally 4 meters side up. The roof is often covered with stone or tiles. The structure is designed to be lightweight, is entirely made of wood and is usually supported by 4 or 6 stone columns of about 1.5 / 2 meters high.

Horreos almost always have a single door that ican be reached by a wooden ladder. The elevation from the ground was necessary to protect the food stored inside from animal raids: mice, dogs, cats and wildlife. As well as obviously by weather agents.

I myself saw the Horreos in Galicia, where I counted thousands of them. In Galician land horreos have rectangular shape, they are usually smaller and almost always made of stone or bricks. They are even enriched by friezes of all kinds, mostly religious.

The Horreos are an integral part of the culture of these regions and of the places you will cross during your Camino: watch them carefully and take pictures of those you like the most: it will be another great memory to take home!

The Credential

A pilgrim can renounce everything: dresses, food, sleeping on comfortable bedding, or else, except one thing absolutely essential: **the Credential**.

The Credential is the pilgrim's travel document par excellence, a document that accompanies the pilgrim always, throughout the pilgrimage path.

The Credential does not only serve to attest the identity of the traveler, but also his condition and intentions. By filling it, he declares to observe moral rules, civility and education.

In short, the Credential serves to distinguish a true pilgrim from any other traveler.

Thanks to the Credential, the pilgrim can find hospitality in pilgrim facilities, in albergues managed by religious institutions (which often accept on payment a free donation) and in all the structures of the Camino.

There is then a typical ritual in the life of the pilgrim, that of the stamping of Credential. In fact, in order to get the Compostela (see next chapter), the pilgrim will make its own Credential stamped at every stage of its journey, which will then become a true testimony of the different stages and the kilometers travelled.

As explained on the site of the Confraternity "the Credential is issued by a religious authority that takes responsibility for what it declares, so it must be used withresponsibility and honesty. It is released by the Confraternity directly to those who demand it and who commit themselves to accepting its meaning and spirit. It is released to those who walk the pilgrimage routes on foot, by bicycle or on horseback".

As to me, I received the Credential in Italy, thanks to the network of the Confraternity of San Jacopo who realized his own Credential with the characteristics indicated and, honestly, even more beautiful than the Spanish one. The Credential free though any donation is welcome. I would suggest you to get informed about the activities the Confraternity manages to help the pilgrims, so you will understand that your support donation is a great way to start your journey.

The Credential issued by the Confraternity is one of the very few not released by the Cathedral of Santiago; in fact on December 17, 2015, the Chapter of the Cathedral of Santiago de Compostela has issued a statement (we can read it on the site of the Confraternity itself), in which he declared that they would recognize as unique Credential that issued by the Cathedral itself. This was essentially the case for Spain, but considering the possibility of evaluating special agreements for the credentials of foreign institutions under of specific circumstances. Since the Confraternity of St. Jacopo has been releasing its own credentials for over twenty years, with the ecclesiastical imprimatur, and working concerning the pilgrimage, the Deàn of the Cathedral of Santiago, don Segundo Pérez López, recognized the validity at all effects of the Credential released by the Confraternity.

As I said, I preferred to retire my Credential in Italy, just to support the St James Confraternity and be ready for my Camino!.

The choice is up to you!.

The Curiosity:

There are people like me who walked for only 5 days, picking up some ten stamps on his credentials, and then there the record man: he is called Alberto Castello da Pereda.

Alberto is a Spanish from Valencia, and is still marching along the European pilgrimage routes since 2013.

Alberto is the man of the record, because in his pilgrimage for peace he has gone over 19,000 miles, and has incredible Credential: 25 meters long for over 1531 stamps collected on the streets of Santiago, the Via Francigena, Loreto paths and many others.

With the collaboration of the Diocese of Gubbio, the Spanish pilgrim will try to be admitted into the Guinness World Record for its super Credential!.

The Stamps (los sellos)

The Credential (we talked about it in the previous chapter) is a document that contains, besides the pilgrims data and the cover page, several white spaces.

The Credential purpose is to identify the pilgrim and witness his passage along the route, and then allow the Oficina de Peregrino to certify the route and above all the kilometers travelled by the release of the Compostela.

What are Credential white spaces for? How is it possible to certify miles walked on foot (which is not a competitive race)?.

Here is the answer: the stamps (sellos) serve just this aim.

Whenever you sleep in one of the Camino facilities, each time you stop for a small break, or at the restaurant for a meal, here's the time to ask the Sello!

Obviously there is no obligation, you can ask for the stamps where and whenever you want, but I would advise you to ask them at every stage you will make, even for just a coffee, stamped chronologically, after writing the date you visit that place.

By doing this, you will not only become accustomed to "certify" the stages of your Camino but you will also build a beautiful "stamped" tale of your walking experience.

Along your route you will encounter stamps of all kinds, size, color and shape. There are many really nice and commercial activities are almost in competition to create the best ones!.

In addition, many shops (bars and restaurants in the first place) often display signboards out of their facilities announcing that there, yes just there, you can find the coveted Sello!.

The Compostela

Here is the reward of the Pilgrim! It is Compostela, the document written in Latin, which certifies your Camino and rewards your efforts.

After walking for days and days, after diligently filling in your Credential with all possible stamps now you have to think about the Compostela.

Once arrived inSantiago De Compostela you will need to look for the Oficina de Peregrino (find the directions in the "Addresses" chapter) and prepare for a rather long queue. In the summer months the shortest queue is ... long!. If you make your Camino from June to August consider to wait for at least one hour.

After waiting in a queue and arrived at the Oficina counter, you will give your precious Credential full of stamps to one of the operators, you will answer his questions and you will get the much-covet parchment!.

Do not worry for your Credential: the operator just looks at it to determine the distance you travelled and then to give it back to you. It's too much of a precious reminder to not take him home, right?.

Well, a part from the long queue, once your Credential has been checked it will take a few minutes to get your precious Compostela: a parchment with your latin handwritten name, where the Oficina declares that you have arrived in Santiago completing your pilgrimage, and so you have all the Pilgrim's chrisms.

Remember that the Compostela is the only official document attesting your pilgrimage, and is released for free.

The Distance Certificate

Once you arrive in Santiago, at the Oficina del Peregrino you can ask the Compostela as well as the "Distance Certificate of the Santiago de Compostela Way" ("certificado de distancia" in Spanish).

The Distance Certificate is a document recently introduced (in 2014) on the increasing demands of pilgrims to obtain a statement of the distance travelled.

The Distance Certificate is usually required along with Compostela and is issued, upon payment of 3 euros, to all pilgrims who are in possession of the stamps needed to collect the Compostela.

This document, printed on parchment paper and embellished with Latin inscriptions with "Calistine Code" miniatures, contains the most important certifications for the pilgrim:

- day and place where the pilgrim began the Pilgrimage of Santiago;

- the distance (in kilometers) travelled by the pilgrim;

- the day of arrival of the pilgrim in the city of Santiago de Compostela;

- the name of the route that the pilgrim has travelled.

The Certificate size is larger than Compostela, is an optional and additional document without religious purpose.

But I think it's a great way to capture on paper the extraordinary experience of a wonderful trip.

In short, in addition to the Compostela, which is free, we have found that for 3 euros it is also possible to have the certificate of mileage, and for two euros also the tube to better keep the documents in your backpack.

With my travel companions I've been joking for days on the distance calculations: according to our calculations (made with smartphone apps, so via Gps) we had travelled nearly 140 km, while the Oficina recognized only 101! Beyond the fact that it seemed just a little bonus, the situation reminded us so much of some certain great events: according to the organizers the participants were a number, according to the police headquarte ... many less!.

Well, I can proudly hang my Compostela on the wall of my trophies (the others will arrive sooner or later …).

The Secret of Santiago: the True Reason for the Camino

In the previous chapters I have told you how the Way of Santiago has as many variants as the pilgrims who travel it every year (not counting the hundreds of thousands of pilgrims who arrive in Santiago without making the Way or without going to the Oficina del Peregrino).

We could understand together how each pilgrim makes his way for religious, spiritual, or personal motives that make each experience different from each other and every Camino experience is unique as a snow flake or a grain of sand.

But now I'll reveal you a little big secret.

The secret I'm revealing you (let me use a veil of irony) is why all the pilgrims reach Santiago (or rather, the reason why they should reach Santiago).

It all comes from an old story.

The story of the Apostle James of Zebedee.

James was the son of Zebedee and Salome, the brother of John the Apostle, and was also known as the "Greater" to distinguish him from the apostle of the same name, James of Alfeo, cousin of Jesus, known as "Minor" or "Lord's brother."

According to what was written in the Gospels and in the Acts of the Apostles, James the Major was one of the twelve apostles of Jesus.

Christian history says that James, together with John and the other apostles, was very often alongside Jesus during his public life, to the point of being part of the narrower circle of his three most trusted apostles.

According to a tradition dating from the period of Isidoro of Seville (around 600 A.D.), James after the death of Jesus made the same choice as the other apostles, left with the mission of spreading in the known world the Gospel, life and word of his Master.

According to this tradition, Giacomo chose Spain for its path of evangelization.

There is no certainty of this trip. The fact remains, however, that after the mission in Spain it seems that James returned to Judea.

In Judea he found death through the decapitation and martyrdom of King Herod Agrippa, around the year 42 of the first century.

The story of James and the Way does not end, however, with his death, indeed. Martyrdom as often happens in the affairs of the saints sanctioned the beginning of his legendary history.

The golden Legend tells that after the decapitation, after escaping and taking advantage of the darkness of the night, the disciples of James managed to carry his body away.

For the seven disciples began a long a journey that took them by sea to the coasts of Galicia and from here, rising up the Ria de Arousa (a splendid fjord where you can find the photos on my Facebook page), transferred the body of the Apostle James arriving at the port of Iria Flavia, a town now known as Padron.

According to the legend, the disciples of James wanted to ask Queen Lupa for a placein where to bury their Master. Lupa was the monarch who then ruled from his castle the land on which Compostela is today.

In fact, while waiting for meeting the Queen, the disciples deposed their Master's body on a rock, that from then on gave way to becoming the Holy Sarcophagus.

The meeting with queen Lupa was successful: the queen accused the disciples of sin of pride and sent them to the court of the neighboring king Duyos, an enemy of Christianity, who imprisoned them.

According to tradition, an angel liberated the seven men from their jail, and during their escape a new miracle happend with the lives of soldiers running behind them as they crossed a bridge.

It was not the only controversy that men had to face. The oxen who gave them the queen to drive the chariot carrying Santiago's body to Compostela turned out to be wild bulls, which, however, miraculously, tamed by themselves along the way. Lupa was astonished by these episodes, surrendered and converted to Christianity; she ordered to destroy all the places of Celtic worship and gave up his private palace to bury the Apostle. Today the Santiago Cathedral stands here.

Hence, information is lost for centuries, at least up to 830 A.D. when the tomb containing St. James' remains would appear as a luminous view to Pelagio the anchorite, allowing it to be found.

The discovery of St. James' sepulcher immediately took on the connotations of the prodigy, such as to induce the Bishop Teodomiro to go to the place of the remains of the Apostle.

After this miraculous event, the site was called **campus stellae** ("starfield") from which the present name of Santiago de Compostela, the capital of Galicia, derives.

Over the centuries that field of stars became a city; that tomb became a pilgrimage place and afterwards the splendid cathedral we know.

It was in the Middle Ages that the tomb became the destination of many pilgrimages, so that the place took the name of Santiago and in 1075 it was begun the construction of the great basilica dedicated to the Saint, attracting millions of pilgrims from all over Europe and the world every year.

This is the secret of Santiago de Compostela, which is why pilgrims come (or should arrive) from every part of the world: St. James' sepulcher.

To embrace the tomb of the Apostle of Jesus.

On the day I arrived in Santiago, I started my day at 6.35 am, walking with my companions under an extraordinary starry sky.

We left before dawn, because our goal was very close, we felt the scent, the exciting appeal of it.

We arrived in Santiago at 10.11a.m.

We took a few photos in the Cathedral churchyard, the time to leave our backpacks at a delivery point (**remember**: you can not enter the cathedral with the backpack, then there are the security controls to pass) and at 10.40 a.m. we attended the religious mass for the Italians officiated in those days by Don Fabio.

Just Don Fabio reminded to all of us, and I share it with you, which must be the real reason why the pilgrims go to Santiago: the tomb of St. James.

No matter, Don Fabio said in his homily, how do you come to Santiago, whether by a long walking or by plane, and then a taxi: the embrace of Giacomo's grave is for everyone, no one excluded.

It's true.

And I must say that Don Fabio's words hit me deeply.

Yet, since either me and you, like to walk, let's walk.

The Arrival!

It has been a long Way, but in the end you came! No matter if you have walked like me for just 5 days (the indispensable trait to get the Compostela) or that you've been walking all over 800 miles away from Saint-Jean-Pied-de-Port.

Upon the arrival to Santiago many people cried, a river of liberating tears for all the emotions and hard experience of an unforgettable journey. There are those like my travel companions who waved the sardinian flag, or who sang for the last few miles.

In the churchyard of Santiago's Cathedral, I could see pilgrims singing, friends hugging after walking together for a titanic experience, couples exchanging a kiss to renew the promises made in the same place years before.

All these people, all these pilgrims, each with their different history, but linked by the same frenzy experienced during the last few kilometers. In fact when you see the distance becoming shorter, the countryside turning into city periphery then in the central area and you see the signals announcing the city center and the distance from the Santiago Cathedral, each pilgrim regain the momentum, the legs begin to go out alone as if they were animated by a new force.

During the last stage and kilometers even the most tired pilgrims, exhausted by fatigue and pain, regain their strength, energy and enthusiasm.

The Cathedral and St. James are there, just one step away from you.

The arrival on the Cathedral's square carries an indescribable, almost overwhelming emotion: your legs have led you so far, you've been tired, sweaty, you have tried a thousand conflicting emotions, you've known yourself as probably never before , and met dozens of other stories.

All that emotional energy you have accumulated along your path (and its preparation) will melt in a moment, and will turn into something new and unique.

You will be happy as millions of pilgrims before you, you will be proud of yourself and the achievement you will take in your heart for the rest of your life, you'll tell anyone about your life.

Now breathe in deeply, fill your eyes with the colors of Santiago de Compostela and the beauty around you. Listen to the sounds of the square: the laughters of the pilgrims, their enthusiasm, their emotion, their thousand different languages.

Enjoy this moment, open your heart and body to the emotions of this arrival: you will never forget it!

You will think later about your Compostela, the mileage certificate, leaving the backpack in an Albergues: now fully enjoy this priceless moment.

After enjoying this special moment, you can go to the discovery of this wonderful corner of the world that is Santiago de Compostela!.

The Cathedral of Santiago

After a hard work we usually expect to receive an adequate compensation; so after a long journey we expect that our efforts will be rewarded by a beautiful scenery.

For sure Santiago's Cathedral will not disappoint you.

Even though it has been undergoing restoration for 11 years, the Cathedral is fully accessible throughout its awasome beauty.

When you arrive at the yard you may be a bit disappointed, as I was, from finding such an important monument completely wrapped-up due to restoration works.

Know, however, that at least the restoration interesting the Facade of the Obradoiro are expected to be completed within October 2017 and should end in the spring of 2018. Whilst the restoration of the Porch of the Glory (Portico da Gloria) is expected to be completed within 2017.

The renovation works of the Cathedral were divided into four phases and will cost over 17 million, most of which are supported by private people, sponsors and Government.

All this without considering that each year the Cathedral management spends over half a million euros for the safety of tourists and pilgrims visiting the Shrine.

I wish you'll find the facade of the Cathedral free of the scaffoldings, because it is a truly magnificent and extraordinary monument.

The Cathedral is in the square of the Obradoiro, which is obviously the arrival point of the pilgrims' journey, therefore its monumentality welcomes them worthily.

Its construction began in 1075, under the reign of Alfonso VI and at the request of bishop Diego Peláez. It was built under the direction of Master Esteban on the remains of ancient churches built to honor

Saint James.

Although it is a reference work of the Romanesque style, the numerous extensions carried out over the centuries have added to the Romanesque base further architectural styles (Romanesque, Gothic, Baroque, Plateresque and Neoclassical).

The Cathedral interior is a Latin cross with three aisles and an area of approximately 8300 square meters.

The High Altar is in Baroque style and surmounts the crypt of St. James the Apostle, jealously guarded inside.

The main entrance, erected by Master Mateo (1188), is decorated by some two hundred figures referring to the Apocalypse and bearing the name of Porch of the Glory. Among these figures one of the most famous is certainly the representation of St. James the Apostle on the divisional column, a figure that almost seems to welcome the pilgrims.

The facade of the Cathedral's Obradoiro is the work of Fernando de Casas y Novoa and is considered one of the greatest expressions of Spanish baroque.

The curiosity:

The monumental facade of the Cathedral of Santiago de Compostela has been represented in the coins of 1, 2 and 5 cents for many years, but starting from 2018 Spain will also have a coin dedicated to Santiago and the Camino.

To formalize a rumor that has been circulating for a long time was the Ministry of the Economy that has confimed that the coin will be available with the 2 euro currency and will depict the image of pilgrim St. James with the Holy Door of the Cathedral. In addition to the icon of the Saint, the coin will bear the words Spain and the year 2018, while in the outer circular part there will be the 12 stars of Europe.

The new coin will be reproduced in a maximum of 300,000 pieces; for statistical lovers it is the ninth Spanish coin dedicated to sites on the Unesco heritage list.

The Major Chapel

If the sense of pilgrimage to Santiago is hugging St. James, then the Chapel Major is the heart not only of the Cathedral of Santiago but also and above all of your journey.

It is here that you will be able to admire the sumptuous main altar. The altar is in Baroque style and was built at the end of the 17th century by Juan de Figueroa.

The altar is topped by a canopy and contains the stone statue of Santiago, silver coated, a work of the thirteenth century influenced by master Mateo.

I told you that the Chapel Major is the heart of the Cathedral and your journey: so looking around, you will see a long queue of pilgrims, waiting for their turn.

Listen to the silence, interrupted only by pilgrims whispering with others, fill your eyes of the glorious beauty of the Cathedral and wait for your turn: you'll go up narrow stairs and get to a tiny space.

When you come here you will really be to the final destination of your journey: you will be close to the Apostle James. Embrace the Saint and kiss his mantle. How short will it be, enjoy this moment.

The Holy Door

The Holy Door is one of the most important and symbolic elements of the Cathedral of Santiago: it was built in 1611 and was opened for the first time in 1666. It is covered with splendid bronze sculptures featuring biblical episodes, and is the door which is open during the years of the jubilee (the last one was in 2010).

The inauguration ceremony of the Holy Door usually takes place on December 31 of the previous year: during a procession involving religious and civil authorities, the faithfuls approach the door and ask the Apostle to cross the threshold.

According to tradition, the gate of the Holy Door is knocked three times with a silver hammer and the faithfuls are asked if sinners are allowed to enter the house of God.

From the moment of the opening and until its closing, the Holy Door is the destination of a constant flow of pilgrims who go there to get the Forgiveness and to embrace the Holy Sepulcher. The ritual, consolidated over the centuries, also contemplates for the faithfuls to cross the Portico da Gloria, which is on the opposite side.

The Portico of Glory

When I visited the Cathedral (September 2017), the main entrance, the baroque facade of the Obradoiro, was closed for the restoration work I talked about before (for the façade the works should end in 2018).

However, entering from here you will be able to admire (when work is completed) the Portico of Glory, a masterpiece of Romanesque sculpture that was built inside the Cathedral between 1168 and 1188, by Master Matteo.

As I told you, when I wrote this book, this part of the Cathedral was under restoration, so I could not fully appreciate it, but I can tell you that the portico is made up of three round arches corresponding to the three sculpted naves.At the center of the main portal you will notice the statue of the Apostle James, while on the lunette you will find the sculptured representation of the court of Heavenly Jerusalem, with the Christ in Majesty in the center, surrounded by symbols of Evangelists, angels and the souls of the blessed. The twenty-four elder of the Apocalypse are represented on the archivolt.

During the Holy years, the Portico of Glory is crossed by pilgrims to leave the Cathedral after passing through the Holy Door and gaining forgiveness.

I strongly hope that the restoration work is completed when you reach Santiago, and that you can admire the facade of the Cathedral and the Portico da Gloria in all their exuberant and majestic beauty!.

The Botafumeiro

The opportunity to see the Botafumeiro in action is one of the greatest desires of every pilgrim visiting the Cathedral of Santiago, which in all respects is one of the main and most popular symbols.

The peculiar spectacle of this censer lies not only in its size (it is 1.50 meters tall and weighs 53 kg), but also and above all because when it is put into action it is swung along the whole nave and almost touches the roof of the Cathedral.

The Botafumeiro is used for religious purposes, linked to the Catholic liturgy and serves to spread incense, a symbol of prayer and veneration to God.

The history of the botafumeiro is closely linked to that of the Cathedral and the Camino: it is thought that the botafumeiro is an integral part of the history of the Cathedral of Santiago since the beginning of the pilgrimages, although its primary function was not really spiritual. For centuries it has been used to cover the strong smell emanating from the many pilgrims who filled the Cathedral and often found there shelter for the night. Think of what could be the effect of hundreds if not thousands of pilgrims after walking for weeks, gathered together in a closed place, in times when the hygienic and health conditions were not like we are accustomed to today. Hence the need to make the air inside the cathedral more healthy.

In fact, the first botafumeiro of which we have some news is that arrived in Santiago as a gift of King Louis XI of France in the sixteenth century: it seems to be a silver container which was then stolen by Napoleonic troops.

The botafumeiro that is used nowadays (on special occasions you will read later on) has been melted in 1851, and is made of silver-plated brass.

The giant thurible has to be oscillated by the "tiraboleiros": there are 8 specially trained men to lift the censer up to 22 meters high in the center nave cross. Thanks to a complex system of ropes and pulleys, the "tiraboleiros" give a pendulum motion to the thurible, making it nearly touch the ceiling of the aisles at a speed of about 70 km/h.

During centuries of use and history some accidents occurred, of course; one of the most famous occurred in 1499, when Infanta Catalina (future Caterina of Aragona) was present and in 1622. On these occasions (and other lesser known) has happened the bad episode: the botafumeiro has detached from the ropes causing serious damages.

Only in recent time the botafumeiro has assumed its proper function, as it is used for the liturgical functions during the following Eucharistic celebrations:

- Epiphany: January 6
- Easter Sunday
- The Ascension of our Lord (May)
- The Appearance of the Apostle: 23rd May
- Pentecost
- The Martyrdom of St. James: 25th July
- Assumption of the Blessed Virgin: August 15
- All Saints' day: 1 November
- Feats of Christ the King
  - Immaculate Conception: December 8th
- Christmas Day: December 25th
- Transfer of the remains of the Apostle: 30th December

Until 2016, the botafumeiro was also the obvious protagonist of the Friday evening Mass at 19.30 dedicated to pilgrims. From January 1, 2017, this consolidated tradition was however cancelled; **a notice on**

the website of the Cathedral of Santiago announced that "The Botafumeiro will not work in the Mass of 19.30 on Friday until new notice."

What about the reason?. It's a matter of money: despite maintaining this tradition cost little more than € 12,000 per year, the three institutions that have always paid for the service (the Chamber of Commerce, the Tourism Office and the Association of Traders) have decided to give up with it.

This is a rather curious fact considering the movement of money (credentials, hostels, restaurants, travels etc) generated each year by hundreds of thousands of pilgrims arriving in Santiago. If we add that many pilgrims stay at least one more day in Santiago (spending their money in the city) just to assist the Botafumeiro in action, the explanation seems even more incomprehensible.

In addition to the mentioned recurring occasions, Botafumeiro is also run on special occasions, such as major pastoral visits. For example, I was lucky enough to see it in action on the second day of my stay in Santiago thanks to the presence of Cardinal Bagnasco in the Cathedral.

After receiving the Holy Communion, I saw the eight tiraboleiros coming, dressed up with their characteristic mantle, and immediately I realized that something extraordinary would happen.

So I approached the central nave, gaining a precious place from which I witnessed the impressive scene of this giant thurible. I can guarantee that the view of an object of 53kg supported only by a rope oscillating on the heads of thousands of people and reaching a few inches from the roof of the nave is a truly unique spectacle.

Tell you a curiosity: you can ask for the Botafumeiro operating during the pilgrimage, just send an email to the Oficina del Peregrino.

From the information I got, you should make a donation of at least 300 € for it. On the Facebook page of this book and on the website you will also find videos that I could take while the Botafumeiro was in use.

The Masses:

Beyond your religious convictions, I think that once you arrive in Santiago, it is imperative to visit the splendid Cathedral. As I told you, I have my own particular and personal vision of religion and faith, although I recognize in these places an absolutely magical power.

I could never get to Santiago without bowing in front of the altar and in front of the tomb of St. James.

I could never have lost the mass, nor the one in Italian language, nor the general for the pilgrims.

I here list the Mass Hours (updated in September 2017) for the faithfuls and pilgrims, including the times of the messes in Italian.

Sunday and holidays

9:30 h: Morning prayers

10: 00h: Chapter Holy Mass12: 00h: Holy Mass for pilgrims

13: 15h: Holy Mass

Saturdays and public holidays eve

9: 30h: Chapter   Holy Mass and Morning prayers

12: 00h: Holy Mass for pilgrims

18: 00h: Holy Mass in Galician language

19: 30h: Holy Mass

Weekdays

9: 30h: Chapter Holy Mass and Morning prayers

10:45: Holy Mass for Italian pilgrims

12: 00h: Holy Mass for pilgrims

19: 30h: Holy Mass

Source: Oficina del Peregrino (updated September 2017)

Obradoiro Square We are pilgrims and we wander together.

We must learn to entrust our hearts to our travel companion without suspicion, without distrust, and look first at what we seek: peace in the face of the one God.

(Pope Francis)

It is the obligatory arrival point, the first unmissable stop for every pilgrim and for any tourist arriving in Santiago: it is the square of the Obradoiro.

Being located in front of the main entrance of the Cathedral is obviously the most important square in the historic center of Santiago de Compostela.

In this square, during the building period of the Cathedral, there were craft workshops (called "obradoiros") of the workers involved in its construction, hence the name "Obradoiro".

On the square of the Obradoiro, in addition to the Cathedral, there is also the former "Pazo de Raxoi", the ancient city hall from 1787 and seat of the Galician region presidency, as well as the "Parador Hostal de los Reyes Catolicos".

Currently the "Parador Hostal de los Reyes Catolicos" (built in 1499) is classified as a luxury hotel; formerly it was a modest Albergue used to accommodate pilgrims visiting the tomb of St. James's Apostle.

When you arrive in Santiago de Compostela and you will visit the Obradoiro Square, sit on the ground before or after visiting the Cathedral: enjoy the scenery of the palaces around you, but above all watch and listen to the arrival of pilgrims from all over the world.

You will hear laughter, moving tears, and the electricity of pilgrims all around you.

The Pilgrim's Office (Oficina del Peregrino)

As we have seen in the chapter devoted to Compostela, the Pilgrim's Office is one of the obligatory stages of the traveller coming to Santiago.

The purpose of the Oficina is to receive all the pilgrims coming to Santiago on foot, by bicycle or on horseback offering them hospitality and information. The office is managed and administered by the Chapter of the Cathedral of Santiago.

Pilgrims mainly go to the Oficina to show the stamped Credential so to pick up the Compostela and the Distance Certificate, but in reality the Oficina del Peregrino is one of the most important institutions of Santiago.

Once there you can find all the information you need about hospitality in the religious lodges, volunteer associations (thousands every year who come to work in favor of the pilgrims) and everything that concerns the city, the Cathedral and the life of the pilgrims.

Another of the most important activities of this office concerns statistics: here are "counted" the pilgrims who arrive every day in the city, and thanks to the information collected the Oficina is able to produce accurate statistics such as those I have shared with you at the beginning of this book (in Chapter **1, 10, 100, 250,000 routes**). Of course, only pilgrims who come on foot, bike or horse are censed while those arriving by other means (plane, car, bus, camper ...) are not detected.

The Hours of Office (updated in September 2017):

From Easter to October 31st: from 8am to 8pm

From 1 November to Easter: from 10am to 7pm

The hour can be extende of one hour on the basis of the influx of pilgrims.

Closed: December 25 (Christmas day) and January 1 (New Year)

The Gateways of Santiago

(Or rather, the little that remains)

For centuries, in the Middle Ages, the gateways that allowed access to the city of Santiago de Compostela were seven and represented the access to the city not only for its inhabitants but also for pilgrims. Each passage-way was guarded by a door.

Then came attacks and wars: in the summer of 997 Almanzor attacked the city of Santiago de Compostela. There was a fierce and merciless attack: the church devoted to Saint James was burnt, and the main gate of the city was laid waste, but at least the invaders respected the tomb of St. James, which was preserved from the total destruction.

According to the legend, after having exhausted the resistance of the citizens of Santiago and having conquered the city, Almanzor forced the Christian prisoners to carry on their shoulders the doors and bells of the church of St. James, from Santiago de Compostela to the Spanish city of Cordoba.

When they arrived in Cordoba, the bells were used as braziers and the gates were used to embellish a mosque, but after 250 years the roles were reversed and the Muslim prisoners were forced to return the stolen doors and bells to Santiago to repair the wrong the City of Santiago suffered.

The Alameda Park

Before leaving Santiago De Compostela (maybe to head forward Cabo Fisterra) do not miss to visit the Alameda park.

It has been designed keeping to the tradition of romantic gardens and is definitely the ideal place to relax after the Camino, maybe enjoying the scenery of Santiago de Compostela Cathedral and the Obradoiro Square.

In 1885 two lions were placed as guards of the park, which is located a few steps away from the historic center of the city and from the Obradoiro Square. In addition to being my favorite animal, the lion is the symbol that I tattooed on my shoulder with the motto "hic sunt leones", but I would say that this is another story!.

The Climate of Santiago

I was prepared for every sort of weather conditions: from the swimsuit (which I got to use) to the sweatshirt and poncho (well yes, even used them). In fact, since I've not been in this part of Europe in recent times I had no idea how the weather could be.

The first thing I got confirmed (I say so because I've read it, but I'm a bit like Saint Thomas) is that actually the weather in Galicia is quite different from the stereotype of Spanish climate imagining torrid temperatures and burning sun. On the other hand, the same goes for Italy: in Aosta or Bolzano the weather is different from that of Palermo, is not it?.

The fact is that, in the capital city of the autonomous region of Galicia in the northwest of Spain, the climate is obviously very much affected by the Ocean.

Santiago de Compostela enjoys an Atlantic climate: basically temperate with humid summers and mild winters. The average temperatures in the city range between 8 ° -9 ° winter and 27 ° summer; temperatures reach higher peaks very seldom.

Rains are abundant and well distributed throughout the year to the point that Santiago de Compostela is one of the European cities with more precipitation throughout the year. It is not difficult to encounter fog even during the summer season, both during the night and in the early hours of the day.

Thanks to the wind that comes from the Atlantic Ocean and to the mountains around the city, the best time to visit Santiago is August or generally summer time. The problem is that everyone knows it, and in August Santiago de Compostela and its Routes are really crowded!.

The Day After

(or the nostalgia for the Camino)

As you now know, I love travelling. It does not mean I'm a particularly original person: preparing suitcases and travelling more or less cheerfully is a passion shared by billions of people around the world. What I do not love at all is to reach my destination but less to return home.

In fact, I consider the trip itself as an unforgettable experience, sometimes even more exciting than the destination itself. The journey is basically a state of suspension and movement, with all that it takes behind. As long as you travel and move, you feel alive. The problem, at least for me, is the arrival.

Usually, when I come home from a holiday (short or long it doesn't matter) I always feel melancholy, in a bad mood, even more moody than usual. For a couple of days, I'm pretty annoyed.

I guess you'll understand the effect on me once in Santiago: for me the Camino was the every day walking, and not the goal itself. Upon arrival I felt great enthusiasm, joyful hours and sincere happiness, the pride of accomplishing a mission even not imaginable in my previous life, and lots of other emotions.

Well, this was on the first day. Then, as we use to say, "the drive chain dropped" and I started feeling what I resumed in the subtitle of this chapter: a nostalgia for the Camino. I may guess it's comparable to something like retirement after years of work: when you were still working you longed for it but now that you're free you miss your job, your colleagues and your every day environment. Well, that's what I felt for my Camino: the sadness that it was over, the achievement of my goal and the awareness that from the next day all the habits, emotions and moments of my Camino would be classified as memories. Weeks for preparing, days of fatigue but also laughter and emotions that suddenly end. It is true, memories remain, and those will remain forever, and of course it is true that even the finest things rightly need to end sooner or later. But that afternoon after my arrival at the hotel in Santiago, it was a very empty moment, a void that only a dinner with paella and sangria together with my travel companions could fill. Let me speak about my travel companions. Another thing that I can't bear are the farewells. The days shared with the people I met on my Camino I lived very strong emotions for the miles, fatigue, skin emollients, patches, lavadora and secadora, pullo y cerveza and else. It was very tough to greet them.

Accompany them at the station, though laughing and joking as usual (yes, a few days spent together on the Camino can be considered like habits) was really a sad moment. Luckily for them and for me, the journey continued. Though differently!.

Cabo Fisterra

You've walked so hard, you've come to the Cathedral Square in Santiago, you've visited it and maybe you've seen the Botafumeiro in action. You have made a rich dinner with crustaceans, tasted the Santiago Cake and you know by heart every single street in the center of the city.

For some, the trip ends here: many return home, others choose different destinations (I would recommend the Cies Islands, in the Ocean in front of Vigo) but a good deal of pilgrims already see the name of the next destination: Cabo Fisterra!.

Every year tens of thousands of pilgrims, before leaving Galicia and Spain, and after walking for hundreds of miles, decide to extend their journey to reach "Capo Finisterre", in Galician "Cabo Fisterra".

Cabo Finsterra is a promontory that extends over the Atlantic Ocean, in the northwest of Galicia, in a trait of coastline with a rather gloomy name: Coast of Death. This stretch of coastline has taken over the centuries this name because of the high number of vessels and boats that wrecked here; even in 2002 the oil tanker Prestige sunk here releasing over 77,000 tons of oil, causing immense environmental damage.

The Coast of Death has, however, harvested its victims not only among boats but also among pilgrims: hundreds have lost their lives in the waves of the ocean in an attempt to end the pilgrimage with a purifying bath.

In memory of the many misfortunes, it is not difficult to find along the coast one of the many crosses to remember the victims of the Ocean.

The name of this locality, Fisterra (from the Latin "finis terrae", the end of the lands) comes from the fact that before the discovery of America was considered the most extreme point of continental Europe, the place where the world known at that time finished.

This convention was however wrong, as Cabo de Nave in Spain and Cabo de Roca are even more extreme places!.

In any case, Cabo Fisterra lost his geographical primacy in 1492, when Christopher Columbus discovered America.

Nonetheless, Cabo Fisterra has remained undaunted for centuries until nowadays, to keep its fascination and mysticism unchanged.

According to the secular tradition of the ancient medieval pilgrims, after reaching the city of Santiago and praying on the tomb of St. James, the travellers continued their journey up to here.

Once arrived at Cabo Fisterra, many pilgrims were seeking purification through the bath in the frozen waters of the Atlantic Ocean and giving fire to the clothes worn during the way. The beaches of Cabo Fisterra is also the place where the pilgrims used to pick up the Concha, the scallop shell symbol of Santiago, the everlasting testimony of walking the Santiago Camino as a whole. However, as I told you before, often occured that pilgrims lost their life during the ritual of the purifying bath.

Walk or not, with the ocean you can not joke.

As I told you, unfortunately I did not have enough time to walk until here; therefore I went to the Santiago train station (it is less than 2km from the Cathedral) on foot and took a bus to Cabo Fisterra.

By bus there are less than 2 hours of travel and the rides are quite frequent and the cost quite low. I made this choice because I wanted to spend a night at Cabo Fisterra, and this was obviously the cheapest option.

If you want to spend only a few hours in Fisterra, there are also tour companies that at a higher price (around 30 €) organize one-day tours bringing tourists up to the lighthouse (the public service comes only to the town, distant 4 kilometers from the lighthouse).

Once arrived at Fisterra I chose my albergue (extremely clean, well-ordered and peaceful), I wore my sandals and enjoyed a walk to the beautiful beach overlooking the Atlantic.

No, I did not take a bath as I had no intentions to challenge the Coast of Death reputation, but I collected the shells (no traces of scallops) that I brought home as a reminder of my extraordinary journey.

For pilgrims who continued to collect stamps from Santiago de Compostela to Finisterre, it is possible to receive the last certification of the Camino called "La Fisterrana" at the municipal house or at the albergue de Fisterra. This certify that you walked from Santiago to Fisterre and reached "el fin del mundo", i.e. "the end of the world".

After a little break and change of shoes I left, again on foot, to reach the lighthouse headland. A wonderful 4km walk along the coast overlooking the ocean and then enter the lighthouse area.

I was so lucky as to reach the lighthouse in time for the sunset, the most beautiful and intense moment of the day: in the clear days you may assist the extraordinary view of the sun fading away in the waters of the ocean. This was another unforgettable moments of my Camino.

Looking at the Ocean, with the lighthouse on the right, you will see (and here taking a photo is a must) the "zero mile" of Santiago de Compostela's journey. This is the milestone that marks the beginning (or the end, depends on the point of view) of the Camino.

In addition to this very symbolic point, the headland of Cabo Fisterra sinks in the Ocean, in a breathtaking landscape, full of history and emotions.

Here, on a rock opposite the Ocean, you will see a pair of bronze boots, symbol of the thousands of pilgrims who arrived so far took off their boots and left them at the mercy of the wind and the sea.

You'll see everywhere small piles of stones under which you may see tickets, letters and memories of the pilgrims who came to the "end of the earth" before you and entrusted their thoughts to the ocean and to the wind.

Now that you're here, it's time to do what I talked about when I asked you which are your reasons for the Camino.

Do you still remember that I asked you, at the beginning of this book, to write about your motivations and your thoughts on a paper sheet? Do you remember when I suggested you to bend that sheet and place it in a safe but hidden corner of your backpack? Good.

It's time to remind where you did put your sheet.

It's time to pull it out of your backpack.

It's time to entrust your thoughts and your wishes to the wind and the ocean.

And whatever happens, tomorrow you will be a new person!.

Bonus: the Cies Islands

I have added the to title of this chapter the word "bonus" because actually the Cies Islands have a very labile and marginal connection with the Santiago Way, but they can represent an extraordinary extra of sea and relaxation at the end of your Camino.

I have already talked you about these islands, which the Romans defined as "The Islands of the gods", in connection with the Scallop Shell and the arrival of St. James' body in Galicia. In this chapter, however, I will talk about a really unique and extraordinary place in the world, to the point of being named by The Guardian as the most beautiful beach on earth (in 2006).

I came to the Cies Islands thanks to my Cammino comrades met along the way: they had planned a couple of camping nights on these islands. As I was intrigued by their stories (as well as the joy of spending one more day with them) I decided to reach them, lucky enough as my return plane departed just from Vigo.

So after Santiago and Cabo Fisterra, a rather hard sequence of bus-train-walk-ferry has brought me to this authentic heaven on earth.

Accessing the islands is not easy, as I said, since there are rigorous limits and if you wish to spend the night there you have to undergo a rigid procedure, but it really is worthwhile.

The Cies Islands are three and are located in the Atlantic Ocean in front of Vigo, the smallest of the three being **San Martino**, while the two largest **Monteagudo** and **Faro** are connected by a strip of sand, the Rodas beach, which forms a lagoon.

This small archipelago is part of the **National Park of the Atlantic Islands of Galicia,** an area that has been protected since 2002, subject to very important naturalistic constraints.

Think, for example, that access to the archipelago is limited to just 2,200 visitors per day and that the only option (subjected to rigid controls) to sleep on the islands is to stay in the sole and very expensive campsite.

The islands represent a unique ecosystem in the world, an idyllic paradise with finest white sandy beaches and crystal-clear turquoise waters, inhabited by a marvelous marine fauna.

On the islands you will find dunes, pine forests, stretches of rugged cliffs and caribbean-like beaches (like **Figueiras**, frequented by naturists) and lots of animals!. Here live some of the world's most important marine bird colonies and if you have the chance to enjoy snorkeling you will find extraordinary seabeds and wonderful fish.

The activities you can do on the islands are those typical of every resort: sunbath, relaxation, beautiful walks on the beaches or trekking on the trails (you may enjoy a beautiful scenery by climbing the island's peak to the highest lighthouse). Remember that you are on an island and here the prices, unlike the rest of Galicia, are really high.

Accustomed to the low cost of Galician life I have been grumbling at the prices of local merchants all the time of my stay on the islands, adopting my prodigious bargaining spirit for virtually 24 hours.

I'm sure you will enjoy much more than me this extraordinary place!.

Beyond the Way: What I Discovered

I came back home. I landed at Bologna Airport just before midnight between Sunday and Monday. Since I left, only 9 days have passed.

Yet it looks like a life. It was 9 days full of emotions, roaring silence, splendid dawns, wonderful days, tiring miles and dozens of other definitions that to put them together I would need to write another book!.

Once back home, I did not have the time to abandon my backpack that I was immediately overwhelmed by my usual commitments: the company to manage, the thousands of everyday problems, the family for which time is never enough and everything else you know better than me!.

In short, a daily swirling of commitments, thoughts to face, problems to solve and time that is never enough.

Yet, coming home, I found something had changed.

That was me.

My way of seeing things changed, as well as my ability to give the right weight to the problems of everyday life. My ability to concentrate has changed, and I learned how to do it on essential things, to give up many things and ephemeral moments.

I learned how to renounce ... to get more.

I've learned that your shoulders can withstand the weight of all you need to live, and that most of the things we surround ourselves, how beautiful and seductive they may look, are often useless and weighs heavily, forcing us to work harder, to run more and to enjoy less.

I learned that the hamster wheel where we run from morning till evening may slow down and we will feel better!.

I recalled that the best way to pursue the goals I fixed, requires to create the necessary tools, which sometimes allow to even exceed one's expectations.

I reminded myself that focusing on my body and on my mind, is the first step to being a better person, able to listen to and welcome others but also protect myself from any who want to overthrow me.

I remembered being a lucky, really lucky person. Just because I can walk with my legs, see with my eyes and use my body, and I'm ashamed of the times I complained.

I found that my body works better than I imagined, and it was capable of bringing me beyond the limits I imposed on it.

I found that walking is good for my body and soul, to the point that I started walking and running as I had never done in my life.

I found that I want to leave again, with my backpack on my shoulders and booties for my feet, to find myself, the world and people who populate it.

I discovered a new Simone, who maybe was just waiting for a pretext to get out.

May be these appears as trivial revelations, or just memories, given for granted. Maybe they are.

It's not my case, as it actually is the legacy of an extraordinary and unrepeatable experience that has changed my life; I am sure (if you will be able to indulge yourself) will also change yours in some way!.

This was the gift from my Camino.

I have found that beyond the Way, if you are able to let yourself flow, there is a better, stronger, more placid but more determined self.

In addition to wonderful memories, the Way has given me new friends, passion for trekking and running, the ability to concentrate more and better.

It also left me this book that I wish to hand over to you to preserve and make grow together an extraordinary experience, a millennial history that is repeated unchanged in the substance every day, that sprouts new feelings and awareness into the souls of pilgrims.

17 Years of Camino

During the preparation of my trip, and later on while realizing this book, I encountered many times Luciano's website, Pellegrinando.it.

As a humble and shy person, who does not love at all to exhibit, Luciano must be recognized as one of the most listened voices in Italy concerning the Way of Santiago.

Not only he has walked through the Santiago routes for 17 years but still contributes daily to spread the culture of the Camino of Santiago thanks to his website, meetings with aspiring pilgrims, intense editorial activity (he realized some of the best known Italian guides) and the thousands of emails he never gets weary to answer at any time of the day and night.

I have to thank him for the interesting phone conversation on that October afternoon, because in the hour we spent talking about the Camino (indeed it seemed just 5 minutes), he transmitted me so many emotions and points of view I was not aware of.

Indeed, Luciano has the Camino in his blood. After walking for a lifetime he met a doctor who encouraged him to inquire about Santiago walking (let's remember that in 2000 it was not so easy to find information as today) and in 2001 he started on the Camino for the first time.

Back at home, he began to build up Pellegrinando.it: in Italy, in those years the online information on the Way was virtually non-existent, so the passion and the desire to share information and news helped to increase the portal more and more.

One day his son tells him how website Pellegrinando.it is in the first position on Google, and the desire to "live on the Path" started growing even more, not just as a walker but as a person "immersed" in the Camino.

To date Pellegrinando.it gathers hundreds of documents on the Path, with information on every possible aspect; think that there are over 500,000 pages viewed each year and that Luciano has personally answered over 30,000 mails.

While speaking with Luciano I have actually discovered that the ways of life leading you to the Camino are actually as infinite as not important. What matters is not why you come to decide to walk along Santiago routes, or how you do it. What matters is what the Way leaves you.

What matters is not what happens on the way (though important are the memories of a limited period of your life) but what happens AFTER the Way, that is, small or large changes that take place inside us, in our hearts and in our life.

The Way calls every pilgrim, even though everyone is called in a different way, the greatest gift is the call itself, being as important as it is followed.

The Way is a great opportunity for spiritual growth, for anyone who can accept the novelties that will inevitably arrive. The Way asks for open heart and mind, willingness, spirit of adaptation, and ability to welcome the new self that will come

Luciano has lived through all the aspects of the Way, also as Hospitalero, a strong, intense, tiring but precious experience. The Hospitalero (in hostels run by religious and associations) has the very important task of welcoming pilgrims.

If for each of us it is not easy to feel welcomed (for distrust and fear about others) welcoming fellows is even more complicated: it is not just about serving, addressing and responding to requests. On the way, welcome has an even deeper meaning, made of friendship, listening, sharing, and witnessing.

Hospitality begins by embracing the coming pilgrims, help all those arriving, give them information, refreshment and attention until the next morning, when pilgrims resume their journey to Santiago.

Luciano is this, a passionate witness of the Santiago Way that has been living deeply in his body and soul for over 17 years.

Voices of Pilgrims

While I was preparing for my first Walk and later, when I started writing this book, I got largely documented, and I met many pilgrims who, well before me, experienced the Way of Santiago on their skin or rather on their legs!.

They are extraordinary people who have not only walked with their feet, minds and spirits hundreds of kilometers but who have told in their blogs, websites and community on social networks their experience on the way to Santiago.

I asked them to share with me and you their extraordinary experiences, to enrich this book with their voices. I just asked three simple questions, the same ones addressed to me by friends, simple acquaintances or listeners of the radio:

- **How was your first Pilgrimage to Santiago?**

- **Do you have a particular memory or anecdote to tell about your Way?**

- **What did the Camino leave to you?**

Like a fair gentleman I start with women' witnesses:

Marika

Www.mylifeintrek.it

Marika's story impressed me deeply: on her blog she tells when, how and why she started walking, and if you are looking for motivation, reading her story will certainly be a source of inspiration.

How was your first Pilgrimage to Santiago?

I left in August 2016, just one month after making my decision. I walked the French Path from Saint-Jean-Pied-de-Port to Santiago de Compostela and then ended my trip to Finisterre. My walk was better than I imagined!

Do you have a particular memory or anecdote to tell about your Way?

After many moments of difficulty due to my poor physical training, I found great people with whom to continue the journey.

It seemed to know them ever since, so much so we used to call us the "Camino family". With some of them I used to dance on music rhythm to make the periphery paths more pleasant; you know, the absurd thing is that when you're happy you don't feel weary.

You're like a bull and nothing can stop you.

What did the Camino leave to you?

The path taught me that I should not be afraid.

There is always a solution, there is always a different way to deal with things, the world is not ugly and bad as it is painted but wonderful.

I also realized I was really strong.

Now I know who I am and what I want: before now it definitely was not so.

It's not easy to explain why I left so in a sudden for my Camino. Therefore, if you want it you can watch my videos and read my story and my travel experience on my blog: www.mylifeintrek.it

Simona

https://fringeintravel.com/

Reading the blog of Simona you will understand why keeping her and her fringe steady is almost impossible. Which is a good chance because it tells of exciting trips and journeys at the reach of all.

When and why did you start walking?

Very late, as it happens to so many of us, with a thousand complaints and begging my friends to avoid that unnecessary fatigue! I was in

Iceland and my friends decided to get to the top just to eat the sandwich. Though I'm always rather discreet, I bothered them from the beginning of our trekking until next 45 minutes without stop!

"You have a lot of breath, isnt'it?" They said.

Then we got to the top where I could enjoy a 360 degree scenery comparable only to a postcard picture. Impossible to imagine it from below.

At last I shut my mouth and I got aware of the meaning and thrill of fatigue and the wonder of discovering things by walking. I no longer stopped.

Do you have an anecdote tied to your walking?

More than a single anecdote, I would have a thousand emotions to tell about and describe for hours: I have pictures, and thoughts, I have the hard work and the joy of succeeding in it!.

For this reason too, I have created my own blog: it is the coffer of my emotions and experiences, which I also share with you, who read this book.

What did you learn by walking?

Being good at times is really easy and having the good fortune to be able to walk in the middle of nature is a privilege you should enjoy every time you can!.

It does not need to be lost, it does not need to find yourself and not even to be religious or believers or mystics ...

It does not need to be iron man or super trained or well trained.

You only needs to be willing to walk and soon fatigue becomes well-being and at times, even happiness.

Then let's me say that walking costs much less than a psychotherapist! Do you agree?.

Mariarosa

She made the Camino twice, also taking care of the hospital. She has the Way in her blood.

How was your first Pilgrimage to Santiago?

In 2010 a friend who longed for a vacation in Santiago asked me to leave together. I did not know anything about the Way but I found it was possible to do it on foot and realized it was exactly what I wanted to do. So, with the backpack on my shoulders (burdened with some stones) I started training on the streets of our mountains.

Needless to say at the end I left alone.

I walked the whole French Way from Saint-Jean-Pied-de-Port to Santiago. I walked for a month and every day for 25 / 30km, so much to get me a nasty tendinitis that forced me to stay in Leon for two days.

I behaved like most pilgrims do for the first time: respecting the pre-established stages of the guides, wake up at dawn to be sure to find the place to sleep in the evening, without not taking the time to visit the pueblos where I stopped; but above all missing to be careful with my body.

Now, luckily, my attitude has changed.

Do you have a particular memory or anecdote to tell about your Camino?

One morning, at dawn and with my front torch on, along my path I met a Korean scared and motionless in front of a donkey equally frightened. None of them was able to move and both blocked the path.

The scene was so funny that either me and other two pilgrims behind me started laughing. So, at the end, the donkey went back on its route and the Korean could resume the Way, although so shocked that he did not even thank us for our unaware help!.

What did the Camino leave to you?

For the first time I faced my physical and psychological strength, resulting victorious. I shrugged off lots of useless overthinking.

As I told you, It was a lightning strike, a love to live in all its aspects, whenever I can and in different ways.

Irene

https://thewalkingmed.wordpress.com/

She has a background made of long studies and walks, that's why she is a walking med!. Her blog inspired my chapter on one of the great dilemmas of the pilgrim: does the Way Make Weight Loss or not? In addition to irony, Irene has tenacity and culture for sale!.

How was your first Pilgrimage to Santiago?

In August 2014, I made the first stretch of the North Route, from Irun to Bilbao. I chose it for the breathtaking views it promised to offer: from the shores of the Atlantic Ocean to the woods and mountains of Basque hinterland: they did not disappoint me at all!..

Spectacular views, picturesque villages and steep footpaths, seldom travelled, are the peculiarities of this route. Its lesser popularity represents a great advantage when you have to look for hospitality in the albergue. Not only that, being few, it is easier to get acquainted with other pilgrims.

Do you have a particular memory or anecdote to tell about you Camino?

Along the way I met wonderful, extravagant and entertaining people but with a certain amount of tenderness I remember a couple of Sardinian pilgrims of a certain age. They left early in the morning but with no hurry to arrive and never losing the opportunity to visit churches and monasteries along the way. In the evening, tired but serene, they took care of one another: a foot massage, bladder dressing, and smiling while agreeing to the next stage.

What did the Camino leave to you?

Being not a religious one, I have experienced the journey as a personal challenge. First of all a physical challenge. Getting up at dawn, walking for hours in the rain, with the mud infiltrating the shoes and the cloak that did not let the air pass through, at the end revealed to be even a mental challenge. I will remember for ever the fatigue, the silence and sometimes the clumsy beauty of nature, but above all the satisfaction that you experience once you reach the goal.

The journey has been an occasion for me to discover my limits, my weaknesses, but especially what makes me strong.

Edoardo

http://www.intosantiago.com/

When I started documenting me about the Santiago Way, one of the first websites I came across (and one of those I liked most) was exactly that of Francesco and Edoardo: in short, they could not be missed in this chapter!

How was your first Pilgrimage to Santiago?

I decided to make my first trip to Santiago in 2013. I started thinking about it in May of that year, when I would graduate. I was weel aware that once I started working it would be hard to find the time to do it completely. Many people had talked to me, some had already done it and they were so enthusiastic. One night in May I made my decision: a friend invited me to an evening outdoors cineforum, where we saw the movie "The Way ".

I felt that it was the right time to do it so I started to inform me on the Internet looking for tips here and there. I admit that at the time I was struggling to find all the information on a single site, hence the idea to build up Into Santiago.

When I started talking to my friends about my journey, they all agreed with my project, but as I defined the route and the miles I had to travel they began to withdraw, until I found myself alone.

At that time I did not know about the existence of all the routes to Santiago so I decided to undertake the only way I knew, the French one.

Me and the French route, September 2013, 800 miles in solitude: an amazing experience.

Do you have a particular memory or anecdote to tell about your Way?

To anyone who decides to walk, I would wish to do it alone. One of the most beautiful anecdotes I remember is one evening when it was raining. I had decided to reach a small town for the night, but along the way I was drawn to a detour pointing to a little church.

I climbed an impervious path and once in front of the church I met a man, about forty, who invited me to spend the night there as there were just two vacant beds.

Although it was not in my plans I accepted his proposal.

In that somewhat hidden place I met Giorgio (a great lonely traveller who walked long and wide through many paths), Luisa (a young mom who decided to walk with her daughter after separation) and Emily (and English girl who undertook the Way just to satisfy her curiosity).

After having dinner together we made a moment of prayer in the chapel, everyone in it own language.

What did the Camino leave to you?

That evening helped me to understand that despite each of us having different stories, there are moments when, even by perfect strangers, we can share ourselves and our humanity with others.

I do not think it's easy to describe what the Camino left me.

I've been thinking so much in the months and years that followed. Why are everyone so excited? Why they all say it's a life-changing experience?.

I think that for some it is really so, that is, an experience from which modifying one's life, for others it was just a nice walk in company.

Personally, I have long sought the original spirit of the journey, stopping in symbolic places, trying to understand its deep meaning and enjoy its spiritual dimension.

For me it was like "living another life", meaning that starting alone I got into a challenge with myself.

I have faced physical and psychological difficulties, I was amazed by the pilgrims met, I listened and told, I questioned my ideas, I meditated, I saw incredible sunrises and sunsets, I dreamed about my destination and I reached it.

Elena

http://www.elenabellini.it/

http://www.elenabellinireporter.com/

Elena is a photographer and reporter. She travels for passion and work and in the summer 2017 she travelled her Way for the first time, relating about it on her facebook page with beautiful photos and poignant words.

How was your first Pilgrimage to Santiago?

I wanted to understand the deepest spirit of the Way, to understand how such an experience could enrich so many pilgrims. I also did it for personal and health reasons, but one day this particular mix has given me the courage to book the airline flight!. I stayed 48 days away from everything and everyone, only me and my house on my shoulders. After the click of the online payment, I felt a deep emotion mixed with fear, but to know that in a few months I would have left gave me a huge emotional charge.

I left alone, I did the whole French journey starting from Saint-Jean-PdP in France, then I crossed the Pyrenees to get to Santiago. Then not satisfied by my goal I came to Finsterra, the "fin del mundo". I have trampled on about 920 km and I still do not believe it. In fact I usually do not walk; I have a big problem in my back and basin, I had 15 pounds on my shoulders, I spent more time to visit pharmacies than churches but I succeeded in it!.

Today I can say that my first Way of Santiago was a direct injection into vein of energy optimism, strength, fatigue, pure emotions, laughters, collaboration, life!

I have been thrown for an indefinite period in another life, with different times, with different priorities, with daily life full of deep breathings and unforgettable moments.

Do you have a particular memory or anecdote to tell about your Way?

Such a long walking brings you to know wonderful people: I left alone, and I immediately made friends. Friendships that go and come in life, who has the fastest step, who is slower, and who has your own time. In the middle of the path I had a serious tendinitis to my right leg that did not allow me to walk anymore. I was knocked down as to think of stopping. Instead, new friends "with my step" spurred and helped me find a solution. They were unknown people, but if I did not have them at my side at that time, perhaps I would not even complete my Camino. They helped me like I was a sister or an old friend and I have to thank them a lot, thank you again ... and thanks to the Way!.

What did the Camino leave to you?

Already before leaving I felt the need to slow down the rhythm of this chaotic life. A life that leads us to live badly, as if we were crazy little pinball balls that forgot important things. The Way has strengthened my beliefs, but not only these, day by day.

The journey made me realize that only those who are steadfast (and have no serious problems) can struggle and reach even the most complicated goal. He taught me to appreciate even more the differences (even if I already have an open mind because of my travels around the world) and do not overwhelm me in the dreary moments or even in the most solitary ones because you are never alone!. The Way Docet!.

Daiana

Tireless walker, web-based multinational manager, the Way changed his life and heart.

How was your first Pilgrimage to Santiago?

It was 2008. I was living in Milan from four years, but mainly during the last one I realized I was not happy at all. I had a job that, although well paid, made me an empty and superficial person: I felt lost. I decided that I wanted to go back and be serene, starting from the less material aspects of life.

Ten years ago the information on the Way was not so widespread, it did not really know what it was and what to expect from this trip; now there are surely more information and documentation about it, and it has perhaps become some sort of fashion for some.

The fact is since years I wished to go the Way and I wanted to share it with a special person as much as the experience itself, at least how I supposed it could be.

I would have to go with my ex boyfriend but 15 days before leaving he changed his mind and a week before he decided to close our relation.

So I travelled with another person, even more special and unique: myself.

Do you have a particular memory or anecdote to tell about your Way?

One of the aspects I remember with greater happiness concerns friendship. As I said, I started my Camino alone: every morning I chose my travel companions or walked on my own. In Sarria, one of the last stages, I met a group of boys from Valencia and decided to make the last days of travelling with them. After a few months I paid a visit to them and now, thanks to the close acquaintance with people who I think are absolutely special, I can say I have been living in Spain for ten years. My life has completely changed, and I feel I have all the elements to be happy: I got acquainted with people of great value, I have a job that compensates me, and I dedicate my free time to sports and social, feeling useful and satisfied.

What did the Camino leave to you?

My life can be diveded in before and after the Way. It was an experience that marked me deeply. On the Way all of us are equal, without distinction of class, ethnicity or language. I found a very high level of altruism in the people I met along the route: I talked with boys and girls who were absolutely unfamiliar, opening up and telling not so superficial aspects of myself. Similarly, I was honored with as much sincerity and openness. In those moments, I became even more aware that life is not only work, money, power, but it is based on very different values, those which are worth living.

I understood that my life goal is my happiness: only with that, in fact, you can build up what you desire more.

Barbara

A family event has transformed the desire to walk the Camino in a pressing need, which could no longer be postponed. With her backpack on shoulder she went off with her partner: the first 250 kilometers were not enough for her, and she is ready to prepare the next Camino.

How was your first Pilgrimage to Santiago?

After a severe family loss I actually turned my desire to go the Way into reality. At first I thought I would leave alone, being aware that I would never be so but then my partner decided to leave with me: on September 16th we left, backpack on our shoulders, Astorga (on the French path) and we arrived in Santiago on September 24th. There have been really hard moments: at least once a day you feel defeated and incapable, you wonder if your tendons are over, find out that you have muscles you do not even suspect of existence, you feel exhausted but you do not stop because you have an energy charge you do not know where it comes from and keep walking without stopping, with your travel companion and your thoughts. We walked at five o'clock in the morning in woods and trails with just the light of a torch on our foreheads, faced exhausting climbs and stabbing pains, but we loved every single step.

Do you have a particular memory or anecdote to tell about your Camino?

250 kilometers are enough to keep in my heart an infinite number of memories: from the boy who gave my partner a band to allow him to continue the journey, or another pilgrim who, seeing him suffering, practiced a regenerating massage accepting in return nothing more than a few steps together. A very special anecdote that I have in the heart is a hostel dinner in Villafranca: the hospistaler divided the groups and the couples to allow everyone to socialize, despite the different languages and cultures. A unique experience of friendship and brotherhood: the desire to communicate and to confront us was so great that we were able to communicate with our eyes and with a thousand gestures!

What did the Camino leave to you?

I came home with a positive energy and an emotional charge I did not know before: I wished I could leave the same day to live every moment again. Walking with a 9-pound backpack, without any make-up, without shoe heels, without anything but the strictly necessary, made me aware that most of the things we use to surround are superfluous and you can live without them. Get dressed in the dark so as not to disturb anyone who sleeps, sleeping in dorms with strangers, walking and eating with strange pilgrims, helping and asking for help taught me a new way of sharing my life with one another. On the Way I felt light, alone with myself even the worst thoughts came in under a completely different way. The memory of those days andfeelings still accompanies me every day. And every day I would be ready to start again!.

Erica

In the summer of 2014, Erica left f with her husband Ezio and her daughter Jasna of two and a half years. A beautiful testimony of the Way made with a little child. The Way has left them something really unique!.

How was your first Pilgrimage to Santiago?

We left Astorga, about 300 km from Santiago. I had already made the Way in the past, but this was the first time with my family: we were two adults (my husband Ezio and me) and Jasna, who at the time was two and a half years old. We carried her with an ergonomic toddler carrier. We spent eleven days to reach to the cathedral. It was a very nice experience, and with a minimum of organization everything went smoothly: I carried the baby, while my husband had the big backpack with all that needed.

We left very early in the morning, and by 12/13 pm we arrived at our destination. The afternoon was all dedicated to games: Jasna was delighted to find a new hostel every day and a new playground to discover.

Once, maybe in Portomarin, we chose to sleep at the hotel rather than in the hostel and even in Santiago we spent the night in a hotel. The possibility of bathing in the tub at Portmarin, has actually entered the top 10 of the pleasures of life!.

Do you have a particular memory or anecdote to tell about your Way?

After a long stage we arrived in a small village on a hill, may be it was Foncebadon. Upon arrival at the hostel the terrible (at least for a mom) surprise: the diapers for our daughter were over. Despair and worry until the incredible thing happens: a local lord takes the car and drive it to go and buy a pack of diapers for our little daughter!. It could appear a little gesture if it was not that a stranger made 30 miles to and from for our daughter!.

Another memorable adventure is what we experienced climbing O' Cebreiro. There was really a bad weather and we only had poncho and wind jacket, but no clean and long trousers for Jasna. Once we arrived at O' Cebreiro, we consider the chance to take a taxi to continue our trip with the baby without proper clothes, who would risk fever the next day!. In the souvenir shop there were not, of course, children's clothes, but my husband had the great idea to buy a pair of long socks to cover our child's legs! Mission accomplished! We left and the weather assisted us!.

What did the Camino leave to you?

Along the way we have received so much help, and even for our little one it was a magic experience: there were people who played with her, who gave her a small backpack, every day a new and incredible experience! In 2014, there were not so many children on the way, but it is an experience that I can recommend to those who want to go to thank Santiago, who has something to ask, who has a bit of adaptation spirit.

By the way, the Camino has left to the three of us the most wonderful gift: once in the Cathedral, Jasna asked for a sister to Santiago and a month later in my belly there was Sanja!

Francesco

http://www.Intosantiago.com

Francesco along with Edoardo runs IntoSantiago.com, a project that through the website and the Facebook page gathers information and advice to best face the Way.

How was your first Pilgrimage to Santiago?

Simply extraordinary. I went on the Camino for the first time in the summer of 2014 (the French one), and again in 2017 (the Portuguese). The first time it was almost by accident: I received an email from a priest friend (of Regnum Christi) that I did not hear for so long. Actually it was an invitation to leave with other guys I did not know.

To tell the truth my plans for that summer were quite different: it had to be a holiday dedicated to enjoy only sea and sun. Moreover at that time I did not even know what the Way was, I was absolutely disinformed about it.

The fact is that reading that email I felt inside me an increasing desire to leave: something inside told me that it would be the best choice.

The months passed and while everyone around me organized for vacations, my fixed thinking was the Way.

So I decided at the last moment to depart for Spain, direction Leon. I had a few days of vacations available, but I wanted to walk on the Way, so I joined the priest friend group.

Do you have a particular memory or anecdote to tell about your Way?

Every day, each step is a unique and particular reminder: they were exciting and crazy days, I knew the story of St. James and the Way, I met wonderful people, seen unique places, lived very strong emotions. Moreover, maybe due to my work in digital communication, but I still remember when walking towards Porto Marin, I got the idea of creating a website devoted to the Way to help people who want to walk it. Hence the website IntoSantiago.com.

What did the Camino leave to you?

One of the wonders of the Way is the spirit of brotherhood and friendship that is born right away: you know people who in a very short time feel really close, almost as if I knew them from a lifetime. This I think depends on the fact that when you share the same goals, like the Way of Santiago, somehow you tie in a way you would never have thought.

Do you know something really? Some people say that at a certain point in our lives, St. James calls. They call it "The Call of St. James" and I think that was just so for me. I can say it was really the best choice I could do.

Antonella

Antonella is one of the walkers I've known on my Camino, a person with gentle feet but with a strong heart, deep and very nice, always ready to be ironic but with deep thoughts.

How was your first Pilgrimage to Santiago?

I went through the English Path in 2016, I did not have a religious vision of the Way but I decided to leave without a precise reason. In 2017 I walked a part of the Portuguese one and I really liked it, maybe for the companionship or for the beautiful landscapes.

The Way has also given me the opportunity to visit Galicia, an extraordinary land.

The Way of Santiago has something magical that I'm unable to explain and if you do not live it, it's not easy to tell. This journey has consolidated old friendship and has created new ones. The walk makes you know people as they really are and that's beauty.

Do you have a particular memory or anecdote to tell about your Camino?

Before I left I was documented, and one thing that struck me deeply was reading about the liberating cry of most of the pilgrims who came to the Cathedral. I still remember the emotion that pervadedto me in Santiago: before I entered the cathedral I had and explosion of tears that I could not stop, a weeping that I still can not explain today.

In Santiago, a girl from Milan we met along the way asked me, "Would you do it again?", I did not think twice and said, "Not even dead": well, I did it the next year. On the other hand, only stupid peoèle do not change their minds.

What did the Camino leave to you?

When you get back from the Way you are stronger, or maybe you were before but you had not the energy to put into practice what you would have liked to do. I think the Way gives you a great energy and the awareness that if you want to do something you have to try it without having so many fears or without worrying about what others will say or think.

You realize that you can live without so many things, and you can still reach the goal we all long for: serenity.

The Way will push you to live in the day, as I love, and leave you a peace that you do not know where it comes from, but it comes.

You walk for miles and you do not know why (at least I did not know) with the blisters under your feet (one in each foot is a slaughter) but you go on and reach your destination.

Although you walk with other people, you spend days alone with yourself, and when you realize that you are not so bad then you are ready to break the world.

The Camino helped me to gain a greater awareness of myself: once back home and in a month and a half I decided to change office, to dissolve a company, to enroll in several courses that will help me in my work and above all limiting superficial relationships. I think it's just the beginning of my change!.

"You leave looking for something, you walk in search of a destination, having a clear goal. Although you can not know exactly what you will encounter along the way"

From the Fb page of **Lisa**

How was your first Pilgrimage to Santiago?

In this world, where everything is always too fast, sometimes things are happening leaving a sign in your soul: through internet I met a girl from Pistoia and decided to leave together. It was the summer of 2014 and I can say I started with basically a stranger. But fate sometimes puts people on the same path, giving birth to splendid and solid friendships. Due to short time available, I've travelled 220 kilometers in 9 days, a short Way but definitely intense.

Do you have a particular memory or anecdote to tell about your Way?

I still bring with me the inner silence that accompanied my days, the noise of the steps, a silence that almost forced you to face yourself, with your thoughts and your heart. It is a silence that we are no longer accustomed to welcome in our everyday life, as often we are not ready to welcome even ourselves and our deepest and intimate thoughts. I was hit by the thin, invisible string that seemed to tie the people encountered along the way: though many times one lost the presence of the others to pursue one's own travel plans, we often met again, perhaps in an albergue or during a break. It was as if the fate kept us close to each other. Along my Way I met a young girl, one of the carabinieri who was in Nassiriya, who only after sharing a long part of the walk with me, she told about his story, incredibly moving. One more memory that will always keep in the depths of my heart.

What did the Camino leave to you?

I came to Santiago while raining, and the morning after my arrival I went to the Cathedral to attend the Mass of the Pilgrim. In the church I heard the voice of an Italian Friar who was officiating Mass for our compatriots and his voice led me up to him. The words he said and the message he left to the pilgrims, though simple, impressed me and represent the deepest memory of my Way. The meaning of the words of the religious was this:

"I know that many of you decide to undertake the Way of Santiago to find themselves, because of the end of a love story. I don't share at all these "new age" ideas. What I can tell you is that the "true" meaning of the Way of Santiago has far-reaching roots. I can tell you that old pilgrims who in past walked all the way, came to Santiago kneeling in front of the tomb of St. James and praying for their own enemies. In fact, the true meaning of the Way is forgiveness, forgiveness for those who want us badly and do not want our happiness. Ths is the true meaning of the Way of Santiago, so make this message your greatest treasure".

If the Way was a gift to me from start to the end, this message was the bow on the gift, the meaning of my Camino!.

On Facebook there are so many pages and groups dedicated to the Way, they all represent a great source of information and news often updated in real time. I take this opportunity to thank Manuele Dalceste, one of the directors of the public group "Cammino di Santiago", thanks to him I have been able to collect (and share with you) the testimony of many other pilgrims.

Michela:

My first Way was just a brief glimpse of a long journey that I'll do in the future. I could only do the legendary and contested 110 kms from Sarria: a very beautiful walk and an unforgettable experience. An inner journey made with two friends from the primary school that I have not seen for more than 30 years: great emotions and a meeting with Father Fabio who changed my way of perceiving religion. I think that, you will not get rid of the Camino after you have walked it at least once; in fact, as to me, it does not pass day without reading a message of pilgrims walking!.

Francesca:

I started without any expectation, without reading any forums, no information at all. I let the Way come inside me and so it was. It has upset my life, I do a lot of effort to move on; to put together these little pieces of this great puzzle that is life!.

I met extraordinary people, seen fantastic places, lived emotions that I thought I had buried inside of me, which instead are pulsing and alive like never before.

The path shakes the soul to make it restless, upsets your heart, enriches you, takes off but donates! I could start again tomorrow, I would go all the while to enjoy this magnificent experience once again. My best friend was with me, with her fragilities and strength, being for me a great example of how constancy and determination can all realize.

And what about Paulo, that boy who held my hand and left a whirl of emotions in my heart to make it like a stormy sea. I think of the constancy of many, of Aldo's tenacity, the deepness of Nicolas, the daughter of Jesus and her message. I think of whoever wanted to be alone or who believed to be and found out he never was.

I think of the Way every day, every day with passion, melancholy, and endless love.

Daniela:

I wanted to make my Way alone, starting with Sarria, but then my husband and daughter allied and the result was that my love became my caretaker!. Obviously I was happy to leave with my husband. I planned to travel only the last km as I did not know my resistance and was afraid I could encounter some pains while I was on the Pyrenees or in the mesetas. My path then continued to Muxia and Finisterre.

I wanted to prove to myself that I could succeed in my intent and I booked a flight for my daughter. On the way back I found that the Way left me a feeling of peace; though the greatest emotion came from my husband when he suddenly told me "I miss the way, while there I felt so good?".

Instead I did not like visiting the cathedral: it looked like the fish market, with lots of noise and everyone looking for photos and selfies. The entrance of the prelates then seemed like a parade and I did not appreciate it, as well as, though understanding the security measures, I wonder why you have to pay for the obligatory deposit of the backpack when entering the Cathedral.

Valentina:

I'm one of those people who for different reasons decided to make the way by stages. Until now I did it from Sjpdp to Burgos and up to here I can say that despite the fatigue, the emotions I felt are so many, so intense and nice that I can say it was the most beautiful experience of my life.

I am a very timid person but on the Path I have found everything: religion, love for beautiful things, and also the ability to gain confidence with people.

I realized that on the Way you can stay alone or in company whenever you want, and I will never forget the acquaintances made along the path, friendships made of smiles, kindness and love.

One night, in Roncesvalles, there was a gentleman next to me who was snoring heavily and underneath a boy who, to make him wake up and stop snoring, whistled all night long.

I remember a Spanish couple in the 60-65 years who walked on the Logroño Burgos section every year and during those days they became for me almost adoptive parents.

The journey has left me the desire to live and above all to feel good about myself: before the Way almost never happened.

I really miss the atmosphere of the Way. My dream would be to leave Palermo on the via Francigena, passing from Rome to Santiago.

My mind travels, the path leads you to think that you can succeed in everything and never break it down: here is why I love the Way and everything that represents it.

Barbara:

My best friend and me started on September 9th from S.Jean, we arrived at Sahagun on 16th, then came home and will complete the Path next year. With my friend I have been sharing values and steps for years, even in everyday life.

My walk was a daily surprise, I thought I would not bear the weight of the backpack but after a few days without my "home" on my back I could not even walk straight.

I was afraid that the combination of my obesity and the ten kilos of my backpack would have annihilated my knees and back instead it was enough to cure my legs every day and protect my knees with suitable knee supports so I had no problem. I was afraid about feet blistering while instead I did not even have one.

I thought that I would meet a lot of people; instead, while never denying a smile, greetings or help, I felt the need to be more with myself.

I have always believed in God, I do not fully share the dogmas of the Church, but along the Way I heard a spontaneous recall, completely new to me.

I will never forget the blessing of the pilgrims in Hontanas and Carrion de los Condes.

I thought that halfway would have been enough for this year; yet I'm still here to cry for missing to reach the ocean, at the "end of the earth" and that magnificent liberating dip into the frozen water.

Although I feel addicted to any kind of junk food, I've never missed the lack of food, though the *café con leche*, the t*ostada con mantequilla y marmalada* and *zumo de narajana* were indispensable to warm my engine.

I usually share my double bed only with my beloved Chicca, a cocker dog, I never expected I would have adapted to a bunk bed.

I never thought that Nicolas, Aldo, Sara, Abla, Simone, David, Chiara, Francesca, Coleen and Scott, Sam, Dani, Paulo, Emelia and Giuseppe, Giancarlo and Luciano, Marie Ellen and Rose, Jesus, in addition to those I do not remember or never knew the names would have entered my soul, though I have only shared with them a few words or a few gestures.

I would never have thought I would have resisted living every day the same actions; actually they were not the same as every day something inside me changed and things assumed a different aspect.

In conclusion, may be I thought too much before leaving and this prevented me from fully enjoying what the Camino offred me but I know the Way is still there waiting for me and I will not disappoint it next time, because he has completely conquered my heart.

Monica:

My teenage son and I have only walked a piece of the path from SJPDP to Burgos: it was strong, exciting and I am happy that my son has fallen in love with the Camino experience.

I remember so many things related to the wonderful people I met. I lived one of the most beautiful moments in Zubiri, by the river side with so many pilgrims with whom we spent the whole afternoon talking, laughing, drinking and eating.

Feeling good with myself and with others has regenerated me.

The Way left me an immense desire to share and conclude what I wish will be the first of so many ways. The best aspects were to live natural rhythms, nature's times, slow instead of frantic, and the essence of everyday life: there were no hours or days of the week, roles, or tasks to accomplish.

The Camino represents the most beautiful, intense and complete experience of my life.

Ultreya! Suseya!

These two words (more the first than the second one) are, like the Scallop Shell and the Yellow Arrow, integral parts of the symbolism of the Way of Santiago. However, unlike the first two symbols (which you found at the beginning of the book) I decided to describe the meaning of these two words almost for the last.

The arrow and shell symbols are the directions leading your body and spirit to Santiago; instead, with these two words we will exchange at the end of these pages the greeting as pilgrims do and I'll wish you from the bottom of my heart "buen camino".

The meaning of both words (Ultreya and Suseya) is closely linked to the Way of Santiago and the pilgrim figure, although their use is now lost. You will seldom hear them along your walking as the have been replaced by a simpler but equally effective "buen camino".

As you can easily guess, both words come from Latin: *ultreya* by ultra (meaning more) and go (forward), while s*useya* could be translated as "upwards".

According to many sources these words appear for the first time in a song contained within the "Codex Calistinus" of the twelfth century, a song that use to welcome the pilgrims greeting them in this way: **Ultreya and suseya, adjuva nos Deus.**

Basically, there are two interpretations that are given to this phrase.

The first figures a meeting on the Way and one asks "Where are you going Pilgrim?", the second traveler replies "I go on (ultreya) and up (suseya) and wish God protect us". Ahead toward Santiago and St. James, up to God.

The second one is a much less poetic interpretation, just a simple incitement (further on, higher) to reach the destination.

Whatever the right interpretation might be (basically we will never discover it) I like to believe it is an incitement to go on one's life, to discover its spiritual heights under the protective wings of God.

But at the end what really matters is that just two simple words have been representing for almost a thousand years an incredible element of aggregation among millions of pilgrims of different ethnicities, nations, languages and cultures.

A simple but magnificent refrain, with which I leave you also thanking for the time you devoted to my book and wishing you from the bottom of my heart "buen camino!".

Ultreya e suseya, adjuva nos Deus

Online Resources:

Before the coming of internet, we used to organize our journey with paper guides, or through the experience of those who had already made the Way or with books often not particularly updated. Now, of course, thanks to the web is all different, and you can find virtually every possible information online.

I've been thinking of devoting this section of the book to online resources that in my opinion could help you not only organize your trip before leaving but also manage you best along the Camino

25 € credit for your next overnight stay chosen on Airbnb.com:

If you have never used Airbnb use this link, you will receive a € 25 credit for your first overnight stay with Airbnb!

https://goo.gl/2Zj2bc

AIR FLIGHTS

Skyscanner allows you to compare fares with hundreds of airlines around the world, as well as hotels and car rentals in just a few clicks. Also find all low cost airlines and all major departure and destination airports.

https://goo.gl/aehKj2

Websites for travel info and preparation:

- **Confraternity of St. James** (https://goo.gl/bjTdTU) is the Confraternity that in (almost) all of Italy distributes the Credential for the Way. The Credential of the Confraternity is one of very few authorized by the Chapter of the Cathedral of Santiago.

- **Pellegrinando** (https://goo.gl/qwGKaV). The portal of Luciano is an indispensable starting point for all pilgrims. Luciano personally answered to each of the 30,000 mails he received. There are hundreds of tabs and documents on the site.

- **IntoSantiago** (https://goo.gl/gyHt8s) The blog of Francesco and Edoardo (they tell about themselves in the chapter "Voices of the pilgrims"), a site full of useful information and tips.

- **Camino de Santiago** (https://goo.gl/2ScwcF) a Facebook group with lots of information, news and beautiful photos.

- **Pellegrini per Sempre** (https://goo.gl/LY4Kgm) is the most important Italian forum dedicated to the Way of Santiago and the most important pilgrimages.

- **ForWalk** (https://goo.gl/rs3ddm) is a beautiful site that allows you to plan, download (or send home beautiful print) the map of your route, with Albergues and much more. The guide is easy to consult and practice to carry with you along the way.

- **Alteia** (https://goo.gl/4iwjEz) is an on-line publication of information, in seven languages offers a Christian vision of the world. This also offers many ideas on the Way of Santiago.

- **TheWalkingMed** (https://goo.gl/pcC7Ez) blog of Irene Campagna, graduated in Medicine and Surgery and passionate walker.

- **Oficina del Peregrino** (https://oficinadelperegrino.com/) is the reference point for the pilgrim in Santiago, with timetables and up-to-date information.

- **Santiago Tourism** (https://goo.gl/nbynn5), the official site of the Tourist Board of Santiago, all you need to know about the city is here.

With a dog or bike:

- Here (http://www.caminoconmiperro.com/de_santiago/alojamientos.html) you can find a list of some albergues that accept animals.

- On **Bikeltalia** (https://goo.gl/AJWpJp) you can find the steps of the official map for the route and dozens of useful tips.

- Here (https://goo.gl/KpU4bX) you can rent a bike on the way.

Almost less expensive than carrying or shipping your own.

• On the website **Movimento Lento** (https://goo.gl/J9anwr) dedicated to the Bicycle Walk, you can find stages (also in Gpx format) and other information for cyclists.

Backpack Transport:

Prices are just indicative, they vary according to the number of packages, weight and item: check before booking.

• **Jacotrans**: is the most capillary and widespread service, operating between Roncesvalles and Santiago. Online reservations can be made. The service is active all year round. The price is about 7 €. jacotrans.com jacotrans@jacotrans.com

• **Caminofácil**: As the former carries out from Roncesvalles to Santiago, online booking at http://www.caminofacil.net/ contacto@caminofacil.net Phone 610.798.138

• **Xacotrans:** One of the most favourite on the French Way, carries backpacks and people from Sarria to Santiago starting from 3 € http://www.xacotrans.com

• **Antzin** carries backpacks and bikes between Saint Jean and León. Cost around 6 € http://www.antzin-mochileros-a-santiago.es/ raullizuain@hotmail.com 686.328.525-669.188.974

Emergency numbers:

• **Guardia Civil** (Civil Guard)   >>> 062

• **Policia** (National Police) >>> 091

• **Bomberos** (Firefighters) >>> 080 or 085 (changes depending on the region)

• **Embassy and Consulate:** it depends on the Country you come from

Thank you!

This book is dedicated to Asia, my daughter, although I spend a little time with her, I would like her know she will own my my heart forever, and I will always walk with her, a step back, but always with her.

After Asia, the first person I would like to greet and thank is you for buying this book and trusting me. I'v done my best to deserve your trust.

From here onwards my thanks are written at random:

Thanks to the people of Galicia, who for centuries welcome every pilgrim with a smile, with a handshake, with a slap on shoulder, accurate indications, a fruit as gift, a glass of water and a magical atmosphere, which will make your Way unforgettable as it was mine.

Thanks to all the pilgrims I met, and with whom I even exchanged a smile, a greeting, a "Buen Camino" sometimes whispered, sometimes even sung!.

Thanks to the new friends I met on my way, who, although they did not know me, welcomed me into the group, the very spirit of this journey.

Thanks to my parents, who have always made me appreciate not only freedom, but also the welcome spirit, the warmth of the family I always wished to have and the fact that, anyway, they are always available fo me.

Thanks to Dario, my brother, who endures my frequent absences and fills them with a precious thing that I often miss:

the ability and the continuity to put order after my passage.

Thanks to Don Fabio, the Italian parish priest in Santiago who celebrates the Mass for the Italians in the Cathedral. He does not know, but he represents for me a great source of meditation.

Thanks also to the person who, though unaware of it, pushed me to undertake the Way: you will be forever in my heart.

Thanks to Valerio Novelli, the author of **"How to Publish a Book or eBook in Self Publishing on Amazon"**. When I was deciding to go on the Way and to write a book about it, he was publishing his book on how to become a publisher of oneselves, the funny thing is that no one knew about the other. Clearly, this maybe a further mystery from the Way.

Thanks also to my feet and my legs, who brought me to Santiago and back home. I'm well aware that140 km are a a short way, but for me they were too many. It is also for them that I could walk my first Camino. Certainly it will not be the last one.

Thanks to Georgia Passuello and the people who helped me to put the rows and pages of this book in order; in fact I go, I walk and write fast, but luckily I have friends who help me to fix my creative chaos.

In the end, thanks to my spirit of adaptation which always helps me to defeat my fears and overcome my limits.

The fact is, as Francesco Busà of Intosantiago.com recalls, quoting Mother Teresa of Calcutta: As long as you are alive, feel alive!.

I AM ASKING FOR A FAVOR:

If you've come up here, I hope you enjoyed my first book, and that you found it stimulating, interesting, complete, and easy to read.

I have devoted all my efforts to publish an easy to read book but with an interesting, accessible, and up-to-date content.

I've spent days looking for information, collecting and organizing stories, data and tips that I hope you will find useful.

In short, I really tried my best.

I'd like you to help me now: I ask you to post a review on Amazon.com, so other people like you can find my book easily.

In addition to the Amazon review (this is really important for me!) I would love you to share on your social page a photo with this book, a review and advice.

I would greatly appreciate it, it would be a huge satisfaction for me to read what you think of my first book!

I thank you since now for the time you will dedicate to me: those 30 seconds that do not mean anything for you, they would be highly precious for me!.

DISCLAIMER OF RESPONSIBILITY

I remember that I am neither a physician, nor a professional athlete but a simple pilgrim, so you should understand that this book does not offer any medical advice nor the purchase is proposed or recommended as medical products: what is written is only the 'the personal experience of the author (who is myself), and everything written should be intended for information purposes only.

The information contained in this book or on the website can not, however, replace the professional medical advice, diagnoses or treatments proposed by qualified doctors.

The information contained in this book or on the website should never replace the personal advice of a physician. None of the information contained herein can (under any circumstances) replace the Doctor's choices, which is always the decider and the final manager.

Always rely on the advice of your doctor or other medical care provider for any questions regarding the medical condition and the treatment of symptoms.

Do not neglect medical advice or do not postpone your research just because you read something about this book or site!

Reliance on the information provided in this book or on the site is only at your own risk. This means that any decision made on the basis of these indications must be understood as personal and in their own responsibility.

The author assumes no responsibility in case of omissions of information, denials, transcript errors or any physical or psychological damage resulting from the erroneous and personal interpretation of what is published in this volume.

The author is at the disposal of all users to correct, improve and expand any content.

BIOGRAPHY

Simone Ruscetta has for over 20 years been one of the most well known speakers of Radio Bruno, one of the most listened radio stations in Northern Italy. Since 2006 he has been working in the online marketing, web publishing and social media marketing. He is the founder of 24media.it, the online Modena24 magazine and other websites. From the experience of the journey, completed in the summer of 2017, his first book "My First Way to Santiago" was born.

My dad Simone in Santiago
(by Asia Ruscetta)

Printed in Great Britain
by Amazon